INCARNATION

୶

A New Evolutionary Threshold

Diarmuid O'Murchu, MSC

ORBIS BOOKS
www.orbisbooks.com

ORBIS BOOKS
www.orbisbooks.com

Fathers and Brothers
MARYKNOLL™

Founded in 1970, Orbis Books endeavors to publish works that enlighten the mind, nourish the spirit, and challenge the conscience. The publishing arm of the Maryknoll Fathers and Brothers, Orbis seeks to explore the global dimensions of the Christian faith and mission, to invite dialogue with diverse cultures and religious traditions, and to serve the cause of reconciliation and peace. The books published reflect the views of their authors and do not represent the official position of the Maryknoll Society. To learn more about Maryknoll and Orbis Books, please visit our website at http://www.maryknollsociety.org.

Library of Congress Cataloging-in-Publication Data

Names: O'Murchu, Diarmuid, author.
Title: Incarnation : a new evolutionary threshold / Diarmuid O'Murchu, MSC.
Description: Maryknoll : Orbis Books, 2017. | Includes bibliographical references and index.
Identifiers: LCCN 2017000402 (print) | LCCN 2017008552 (ebook) | ISBN 9781626982352 (pbk.) | ISBN 9781608337002 (e-book)
Subjects: LCSH: Incarnation. | Faith.
Classification: LCC BT220 .O115 2017 (print) | LCC BT220 (ebook) | DDC 232/.1—dc23
LC record available at https://lccn.loc.gov/2017000402

Contents

Introduction

Humans are on Earth like beings stricken with amnesia.

—Plato

This book offers a deeper set of reflections on the challenges of adult faith development as previously outlined in my books, *Adult Faith* (2010) and *The Meaning and Practice of Faith* (2014). Why are adults in the twenty-first century seeking new articulations of faith, some of which mark substantial departures from church teaching and practice? And what are these adults seeking as alternatives to mainstream religion?

I offer a response to these questions by a more detailed assessment of how *Incarnation* is understood by contemporary adult faith seekers. While the historical Jesus continues to be a central inspiration for adult faith in our time, Incarnation is not restricted to the Christian context. Rather Incarnation names and celebrates the embodiment of God in the whole creation, celebrating what God creates throughout the 13.7 billion years of evolution and beyond that into deep time.

And true to the spirit of mysticism across the ages, for contemporary adult faith seekers, these enlarged horizons do not undermine faith in a personal God, nor the intimacy of the divine–human relationship. To the contrary, it deepens and expands the horizons of faith, even in its deeply personal meaning.

This new exploration of faith requires a radical rethink, with a fresh appraisal of what faith engagement looks like. It requires a new language and an expansive horizon of investigation beyond the more rational and linear approaches of classical metaphysics, and the ideological concerns that often preoccupy formal religion.

This book is an attempt at naming—and explaining—what these new horizons look like. Dislocating and disturbing though some of these insights might be, they offer promise and hope for faith life in the twenty-first century. And to the fore in that endeavor is a cohort of wise elders, largely unacknowledged and overlooked by mainline religions. In solidarity with these aging spiritual seekers, we embrace this faith-filled journey of exploration.

Chapter 1

Incarnation for Adult Faith

All around us we can see men and women throwing off their stereotypical roles, refusing to be slaves of assigned identities.

—Theodore Roszak

There is definitely something spiritually counterintuitive about this business of incarnation, and to really get what's at stake in this mystery, is for me the acid test as to whether you understand what Christianity is all about.

—Cynthia Bourgeault

This book seeks to offer an expanded understanding of the Christian notion of *Incarnation,* drawing on the multidisciplinary wisdom of the twenty-first century. It transcends many of the criteria that define truth within a formal Christian context and seeks to speak to spiritual seekers rather than those committed to one or another Christian denomination.

In writing this book, I have in mind a very specific audience. The envisaged readership is that of mature adults (the sixty plus generation), intellectually curious (not necessarily with an academic background), spiritual explorers (uneasy with the dogmatism of formal religion), and seeking a forum where their exploration of faith can become the subject of serious and reflective dialogue. Many will still be churchgoers but tend not to look to a formal church or religion for the serious and fruitful deepening of their faith.

I detect among this group many wise elders, with an enormous contribution to offer for the future evolutionary development of faith and religion. While I admire the efforts of those who seek to pass on faith to our young people (children, teenagers, young adults), my fundamental conviction as a social scientist is that it is *the wise elders* who will prove to be the primary catalysts in recreating a more credible and empowering faith for the twenty-first century. This conviction is shared by a range of contemporary Western researchers, notably Robert Atchley, Susan McFadden, David Moberg, Harry R. Moody, and Holly Nelson-Becker (cf. Kimble and McFadden 1995, 2003).

It is also my perception that it will be the wise elders who will make the developmental and transformative difference, not merely in Christianity but in all the great religions. Thus far, none of the religions have consciously adopted this option; all are trying to ensure that the youth are on board, widely perceived to be the hope of the future.

It will be the wise elders who will provide a surer pathway to the future, and in this regard I endorse the seminal research of the late cultural historian, Theodore Roszak (2001, 2009). Noting that the world population is growing older at a rapid rate, and seeking to discern the significance of that trend, Roszak was one of the first to note that by 2020 we will have more people on the planet over the age of sixty than under sixteen for the first time ever. Although predominantly a Western phenomenon, the human species is growing older throughout the entire planet. By 2050, all major areas of the world except Africa will have nearly a quarter or more of their populations aged sixty or over (according to the United Nations Report: *World Population Prospects: The 2015 Revision Key Findings and Advance Tables*). People are living longer (despite some blatant deprivations in parts of our world), and when living conditions improve, even marginally, less babies tend to be born. Thanks to improved medical conditions, life expectancy has improved considerably, shifting from an international average of forty-eight years to sixty-eight years in the five-year period of 2005–2010.

The sociological and cultural implications are substantial and remain largely unexplored. In the near future, in Europe and the United States, the primary consumer/purchaser will be an older person. The impact on social policy, economic values, and political strategies is likely to be transformative beyond several current expectations. And all these dimensions cocreate the spiritual synthesis which is becoming increasingly transparent in the lives of wise elders.[1]

Shift to the Adult

Passing on the faith—through home, school, and church—has long been associated with the faith formation of children in the home, and the catechizing of youth through schools and parishes. The goal seems to be quite a pragmatic one: ensure they are well formed and informed by the age of eighteen, and hopefully that will engender a degree of commitment that they will carry with them into their adult years.

It is something of a utopian dream, which increasingly does not work (at least in Christian cultures). In several Western

---

[1] One detects this spiritual transformation in the nineteen narratives of older people gathered and edited by Kathleen Montgomery (2015). All happen to be universal Unitarians, but their vibrant sense of faith is not dictated by, nor confined to, any one church or denomination. This group also represents a growing movement in the United States (and elsewhere) known as "Sage-ing for Age-ing," captivating a mystical vision, yet one that is deeply grounded in real life; Ron Pevny (2014) and Robert L. Weber and Carol Orsborn (2015) provide useful overviews. The more scholarly research into this emerging phenomenon is synthesized by Holly Nelson-Becker (2009, 2011), professor of social gerontology at Loyola University, Chicago.

countries, youth lose interest in religion and religious practice even in early adolescence. More importantly, developmental psychology, and specifically the study of faith formation for various life stages (cf. Fowler 1981; O'Murchu 2014b), highlights a shift in recent decades that most churches and formal religions are either unaware of, or choose to ignore.

Growth into human maturity no longer follows the linear line so long assumed in psychology and pedagogy. Traditionally we have exalted the formative years of early childhood, on the understanding that the behavior patterns imprinted during that time become foundational for subsequent development throughout the entire lifespan. Furthermore, according to this linear view, human character formation is deemed to be complete by the age of eighteen; at that stage, we tend to assume that key personality patterns are solidly set and thereafter will not be easy to change. In this paradigm of human development, little or no attention is given to the adult years, from twenty through to seventy/eighty. Adult behavior is assumed to be largely if not totally based on the earlier formative years.

Nobody can deny the enduring significance of childhood influences along with their impact on later growth and behavior patterns. However, we now know that those foundational patterns can be changed and even modified significantly into old age. It is broadly true that the challenges for behavior modification become more difficult as a person grows older, but that too varies enormously depending on other cultural or environmental influences. Adolescence is still quite a controversial area. We all know teenagers who can achieve a remarkable degree of maturity and psychological integration by age eighteen, but this is quite rare.

Adolescence is a time for rebellion and the restless movement toward an individual identity; contemporary developmental psychology suggests that engaging and channeling such rebellion rather than trying to eliminate it is the formative challenge for healthy growth. Moreover, experience indicates that the experimental nature of the teenage years now extends into what we used to call the young adult, sometimes prevailing into the late twenties or early thirties. Culturally, we still expect the young adult to be fulfilling the three major thresholds of (1) self-reliance in managing money, (2) a serious monogamous relationship, and (3) a lifelong career. Increasingly we find that young adults in the twenty-first century do not achieve those goals.

We need a more discerning analysis of the complex nature of life for young adults in our time. Some developmental psychologists consider this the most problematic and challenging of all the life stages that people go through. We are dealing with the age group constituting the twenty- to thirty-five-year-olds, known today as *emerging adulthood* (Arnett 2014). The process of maturation, one time considered to be well advanced by one's eighteenth birthday, now takes several years longer. This is partly due to cultural shifts such as that of permanent jobs giving way to contract labor (without a permanent workplace, salary, or pension scheme) or the fluid world of human sexuality and relationships wherein the monogamous heterosexual option is no longer the norm. And with such changes come huge insecurity, sometimes associated with societal or parental expectations.

During the emerging adult stage, religious practice tends to be abandoned (predominantly in the West), and when it is assumed, it frequently is articulated in fundamentalist expression. And this excessive fervor can veer toward extremes of social or political bigotry, as evidenced in groups like ISIS (ISIL) constituted largely by people in the twenty to thirty-five age bracket, or, alternatively in a dramatic opt out such as suicide, which also has its highest prevalence in the twenty to thirty-five age group.

Pastorally and psychologically, in the adult realm of adult development, this is the group needing the most urgent attention. In society generally, there prevails a rather naïve set of expectations. These young adults are viewed as strong, healthy, and intelligent; life is there for the taking. Let them get themselves trained for suitable work, learn to make money, and get on with it! And if they run into problems (which happens with increasing frequency), let them sort themselves out, and if they feel the need to move back into the family home, that is fine as long as they don't stay around too long. As for the fluid and irregular trends in sexual behavior and more intimate living, that is an area where most contemporary adults do not wish to be involved. They don't really understand what is going on and are afraid to look too closely, so the emerging adults are left to plod along as best they can.

Despite the great urgency that this subgroup needs—and deserves—they do not constitute my primary focus in the present work; and therefore, I leave the challenge to others, hopefully more versatile and competent than I am to explore some empowering possibilities for our emerging adults. Another life-stage group that will not concern us in this study are the midlifers (approximately thirty-five to fifty-five). Ever since the 1970s, this group has been the subject of comprehensive study, analysis, and discernment.

Classifying Our Elders

When the American developmental psychologist James Fowler (1981) first outlined his stages of faith development, he moved from consideration of midlifers straight into his treatment of the elderly, the universalizing stage that he postulated for anybody from forty-five years onward, a development attained by the rare few. Other researchers, notably, Susanne Cook-Greuter (1994, 1999), Bill Plotkin (2008), and Kenneth Stokes (1982) provide a more refined analysis of this final stage. Plotkin divides it into two stages (early and late elderhood), as I do in my own research (see O'Murchu 2010, 2014b).

In the closing decades of the twentieth century, many people were offered the option of early retirement (from fifty-five onward), and since many of these people were still healthy and active (in every sense), opportunities were sought to reemploy their talents and resources. One significant outcome of this emergence was the University of the Third Age (popularly known as UTA or U3A). Today this educational facility, reserved for the over-fifties, accommodates an estimated ten million people in the Americas, Europe, Australia, India, and China. The popular prejudicial perception of older people being unemployable, nonproductive, a drain on financial and health resources, quickly changed, although much awareness raising still needs to be done.

Beyond early retirement (fifty-five plus) a further life stage requires renewed attention, namely, those over the age of seventy. In religious terms, this subgroup is assumed to be in declining health and are thus admonished to do penance and prepare to meet God in death and judgment. In the Hindu faith, the elderly devotee is even encouraged to leave home and family, and assume a life of greater austerity and simplicity, for example, *vanaprastha* (forest recluse) and *sanyasi* (complete renunciation).

In the 1970s, a revitalization of the notion of the wise elder came to the fore, with Fowler's characteristic of *universality* evoking the attention of various researchers. Despite its scholarly limitations, the pioneering work of James Fowler (1981) still remains seminal. Initially a Western development, it has now become much more widespread, with implications for the global consciousness of our time and particularly its spiritual (mystical) implications (comprehensively reviewed in the *Journal of Religious Gerontology*, initially launched in 1984). Two critical factors come into play here. The first, already noted, is what Theodore Roszak (2001) calls the longevity revolution, with the elderly becoming not merely numerically stronger in population terms, but also becoming a determining political and economic force as I shall indicate shortly. Second, as hinted in the opening quote, the information explosion has had, and will continue to have, a major influence on these older people. While they don't exhibit the dexterity of the young nor their fascination with modern information technology, they imbibe the newly emerging consciousness for *interconnectedness, wholeness, and universality.* They become curious and eager to learn more; their intuition is freshly awakened, and their imaginations are stretched in the direction of expansion, universality, characteristics of consciousness in our time with some significant theological implications as illustrated by the Australian theologian Anthony J. Kelly (2015).

Because our dominant culture is so antiaging (except for the technological compulsion toward perpetual youthfulness, and the end of dying) and largely dismissive of the elderly as useless and nonproductive, unfortunately only limited research has gone into the alternative phenomenon I am highlighting. I know from personal experience that an alternative elder culture is arising (rapidly and universally), and in a matter of a few decades, it will exert substantial influence on our global value systems.

We are rapidly approaching the critical threshold when in several Western countries the elderly will become (1) the dominant voters, much more critically aware of political policies, and not easily lured to support the inherited party system; and (2) the dominant purchasers, whose buying options will not be determined by popular fashion or commercial spin, but by aesthetic, ecological, and more responsible values. Thanks to the preponderance of these older consumers, sustainability in values and practices is likely to expand significantly requiring major changes in marketing, advertising, and consumer practice, the demands consistently upheld by Democratic candidate Bernie Sanders in the run up to the 2016 US presidential election.

My interest in this new subgroup is mainly spiritual and religious in nature. This subgroup is already redefining several aspects of Christian faith, including the notion of Incarnation, the specific focus of this book. These elders (which I define as aged fifty-five plus) come mainly from formal religious backgrounds, tend to be well educated, and often belong to the middle to upper class. However, they question almost everything in their inherited faith and wish to stretch spiritual understandings far beyond conventional religious belief. They perfectly fit Petrim Sorokim's *restless middle classes,* which Sorokim (1950) considers to be the primary catalysts of evolutionary change. And in their expansive vision, they seek to outgrow the dualistic split between sacred and secular; for them, sacredness is universal and predates religion by billions of years.

Spiritual Seekers of the Twenty-First Century

In terms of the target readership of this book, there is an additional group with very similar understandings to those attributed above to the wise elders. The constitution of this group is complex and, to date, has been poorly researched. They can be from any age group, but predominantly are post midlifers. Some were brought up in a religious environment, but many were not. They do not belong to any one social class or economic ideology, although politically they tend to be left of center and passionate about issues of justice and planetary well-being.

They exhibit a distinctive intellectual stance. Even if they come from an academic background, they tend to be critical of what they perceive to be the narrow focus of much academic learning. They cherish and strongly promote intellectual development, which they do not identify with academic achievement. They tend to exhibit a double hermeneutic of suspicion. They distrust all major institutions and tend to be dismissive of the formal teaching of either church or formal government. And they are equally suspicious of academic rhetoric. They seek truth from within a *peer* context, the structural shape of which often feels nebulous but strikes me as being remarkably similar to the church's notion of the *sensus fidei* (sense of the faith), otherwise named historically as the *sensus fidelium* (sense of the faithful).[2]

---

[2] For several contemporary theologians the notion of *sensus fidei/fidelium* is linked with the vision of the Second Vatican Council (1962–65). Before the nineteenth century, *sensus fidelium* appeared in texts on theological sources, but the concept was not employed commonly in theology. The authoritative source usually cited is that of Melchior Cano's (d. 1560) *De*

Applying the label *post-Christian* to such seekers is inappropriate and even irresponsible. Many, in fact, have Christian affiliation with various levels of allegiance to church practice. Much more important however is their commitment to the values of the New Reign of God (the Kingdom): love, justice, compassion, liberation, inclusivity. They may not confess Jesus as Lord (as evangelicals require), but they live out a quality of faith that would put many religious practitioners to shame. Orthopraxy rather than orthodoxy is their primary concern.

In the cosmopolitan vison of the philosopher Jason Hill (2000), these seekers may also be described as posttribalism, and for such people, "Reality has been grossly misinterpreted, and those who detect the cognitive aberrations or, worse, those who figure out what the correct interpretation is, are labelled confused, paranoid, whiners, complainers, race obsessed, and trouble-makers" (Hill 2000, 70). In other words they do not fit into the conventional religious or cultural paradigms. In the past they were more readily dismissed or suppressed, but not any-

----

Locis Theologicis. Cano lists four criteria to establish whether a doctrine or practice belonged to apostolic tradition of the church, including the "present common consent of the faithful" as one of the four criteria. In other words, if there was a broad consensus and reception of a new doctrine within the life of the church, that would reflect the *sensus fidei/fidelium.* Cano suggested that central issues such as apostolic succession, the canon of Scripture, the acceptance of the Roman See reflect this broad consensus.

The renowned Dominican scholar, Yves Congar claims that since the early eighteenth century, the teaching authority of the church claimed a monopoly of truth that progressively undermined the notion of the *sensus fidei/fidelium*, and Vatican II's definition of the church as "The People of God" has initiated a corrective to this virtual marginalization of the "faithful." Another significant name is that of Cardinal John Henry Newman who spoke of a wisdom deep in the bosom of the mystical body of Christ challenging the church to become a "community of phronesis (practical wisdom)." The emphasis shifts to the whole church as a discerning body. The Vatican's International Theological Commission issued a document in July 2014, "Sensus Fidei in the Life of the Church," exploring aspects of the concept and how bishops might apply it in certain circumstances.

more. Although often viewed as marginal, they actually occupy a more middle ground, providing a ferment that can no longer be easily dismissed or suppressed.

Therefore, the envisaged readership of this book consists of two interrelated groups:

- *Wise elders*, that is, the section of the older human population seeking to explore a more expansive understanding of faith and religion, incorporating multidisciplinary insights from a range of different disciplines and from a broad base of human experience (see Pevny 2014; Weber and Orsborn 2015).
- Spiritual seekers, attracted to the evolutionary unfolding of spiritual and religious wisdom in the contemporary world, including the various world religions, but also the spiritual awakening taking place in a range of contemporary cultural settings (see Johnson and Ord 2012).

The Incarnational Focus

The Christian concept of Incarnation has changed dramatically since the mid–twentieth century. Long associated with the coming of Jesus to rescue and redeem humanity, Incarnation described the unique way in which the historical Jesus was born, grew up, ministered publicly, was crucified, and rose from the dead. And no other religious leader achieved that outcome as perfectly as Jesus who, therefore, has been declared as the Savior not just of Christians but of all humans.

In the inherited paradigm, only humans matter. The focus is exclusively anthropocentric. Throughout the latter half of the twentieth century, this anthropocentric focus became problematic. Why humans only, and why only the soul of the human? Attention shifted to the whole person and not merely the ensouled dimension. And since humans have to negotiate their journeys of faith as embodied beings, perhaps we need to give closer attention to our embodied selves. Thus, Incarnation became equated with *embodiment* and not merely a preoccupation of the soul within the body.

Influenced by the growing corpus of multidisciplinary wisdom, the identification of Incarnation with bodily unfolding moved in three significant directions: relational identity, the sensuous body, and transhuman embodiment.

Relational identity is mainly a psychological development with the Israeli/French psychoanalyst Bracha Ettinger (2006) to the fore. While the patriarchal preoccupation (from Aristotle through to Freud) is that of the infant separating from the maternal womb in order to realize an autonomous individualized identity, Ettinger's *matrixial transsubjectivity* claims that the growth process in the mother's womb is characterized by a foundational pattern that Ettinger names as subjectivity-as-encounter. This foundational and enduring pattern means that from our earliest formative moments, we are programmed for relationship, not for fierce competition leading to robust individualism. This psychological insight, supported by theorists, such as Nancy Chowdrow, Lucy Irigary, and Julia Kristiva (to name but a few), has been adopted by several feminist theologians, notably, Grace Jantzen, Carter Heyward, and Lisa Isherwood. For a more detailed overview, see Lyons (2015).[3]

The sensuous body. Christian theology exhibits a long allegiance to the patriarchal anthropology of classical Greek times,

---

[3] I ask the reader's forbearance for frequently revisiting and developing afresh this foundational phenomenon of *relationality*. From my perspective, it is the heart and soul of all reality, human and nonhuman alike, and consequently will be highlighted as the neglected and underrated dimension of Incarnation as understood for much of Christian history. Of course, the foundational relationality I am seeking to reclaim in this book is much bigger than Christian belief. On the microscopic scale, it seems to underpin the world of quantum reality (cf. Rovelli 1996), and on the grand macrolevel, we see it at work in the religious concept of a Trinitarian God (La Cugna 1991; Fox 2001), equivalents that are discernible in other world religions (Panikkar 2006).

inherited mainly through Aristotle.[4] Here the heavy emphasis is on rationality, individualism, and the superiority of the male. Correspondingly, the emotions, the senses, subjective human experience, interactive behavior, and the womb formation of the female is not merely subverted, but for much of Christian history, these other dimensions were demonized. Particularly in the psychosexual realm, widespread repression ensued, leading to our contemporary cultural landscape where the outpouring of repressed sexualized energy explodes all around us. The awaited integration is a daunting cultural task, with theology confusedly struggling on how to embrace the whole person and not merely the rational, ensouled dimension. How then do we revisit and reinterpret our primordial Christian story—the incarnated Jesus—so as to include rather than dismiss all these other God-given dimensions of our incarnational identity? Hopefully, the reflections of the present work will go some way to offering an answer to that question.

Transhuman embodiment. For the multidimensional human body to grow and flourish, it needs the contextualization of the other bodies to which humans belong, especially the earth and cosmic bodies. In the words of the quantum physicist Lothar Schafer (2013, 76), "The inner potential in you is cosmic. When you actualize your potential, the cosmic wholeness is actualizing in you. You could say you are an embodiment of cosmic potentiality." Increasingly, spiritual development is viewed as interrelated with the well-being of all the other creatures that share the web of life with us. Today, many more Christians are asking, "Why judge the spiritual significance of other embodied life-forms in terms of the human?"

Perhaps they have spiritual and theological meaning in their own right (cf. Deane-Drummond 2014; Johnson 2014)! Should

---

[4] The patriarchal consciousness/culture alluded to many times in this book predates Aristotle by at least five thousand years. Carol P. Christ (2016) provides a useful overview, clarifying the various uses of the term employed in this work.

we not be considering these other embodied forms as divine incarnations as well? After all, God first appeared in the body of the universe, and in a vast range of embodied forms long before identifying with humanity!

Thus, we come to the present time and the new horizons being explored in this book. Today *Incarnation is a term with multiple meanings* in the face of which the inherited Christian identification with the historical Jesus seems dangerously anthropocentric and loaded with historical baggage which feels increasingly meaningless for the envisaged readership of this book.

Returning therefore to my target audience, and keeping in mind this expanding horizon within which we understand Incarnation today, the scholarly sources already referred to suggest that the following are some of the key characteristics that our readership will wish to examine anew:

- A distrust of all patriarchal intuitions and institutions and the dogmatic assertions associated with such wisdom, whether of a political, economic, social, or religious nature.

- A desire for a more egalitarian discernment on what constitutes truth, within and beyond the human person, in the evolving context of the twenty-first century (see more on the evolutionary perspective in Chapter 2).

- A desire to include the whole of God's creation in theological deliberation, with specific attention to the experiential dimensions, as we seek to transcend the inherited dualistic divisions of earth v. heaven, body v. soul, matter v. spirit.

- A mystical attraction to the God who inhabits all creation (even its destructive paradoxical dimensions) along with a desire to de-genderize the patriarchal God, favoring instead the empowering ubiquitous Spirit (described by First Nations, indigenous peoples, as the Great Spirit).

- Viewing the incarnational presence of God in all the embodied forms that constitute the web of life, from the cosmic to the bacterial, from the macro to the micro expressions.

- In the Christian context, Jesus is viewed as an exemplary embodiment of that incarnational process, particularly in its human articulation, and lived out in systemic terms through the project known as *the Kingdom of God,* through which empowering embodiment infiltrates every sphere of personal and global existence.

- The personal relationship with God unfolds in conjunction with the multifaceted nature of our human embodiment, forever seeking deeper alignment with the divine embodiment of all creation. We cannot love God without loving God's creation. The personal and interpersonal challenges are developed in Chapter 6.

- Justice becomes the primary Christian response, seeking to establish the right relationships (righteousness) through which all the embodied creation can continue to grow into the empowering and liberating truth desired in God's evolutionary initiative, a process considered to be infinite in terms of space time.

- Formal religion or church organization has a questionable value. Community faith structures are deemed to be essential, but with a degree of fluidity, flexibility, devoid of hierarchal control, close to what seems to have been the nature of early Pauline Jewish–Gentile communities, and embodied in the more recent development of basic ecclesial communities.

- God's revelation is considered to be in the whole of creation and its evolving processes. Each religion exhibits a particular expression of that revelation, one that is dictated by the context of time and culture. And divine revelation is mediated primarily through the embodied processes that facilitate growth and flourishing—in *every aspect* of God's creation.

- The human need for ritual is viewed as the prototype for all worship and sacramentality. It is not needed to placate or beseech God, since collaboration and cocreation with God is deemed to be the basic stance of authentic faith. Ritual entails celebration of God's embodiment in all creation, animate and inanimate alike.

No doubt, critics will see facets of almost every heresy that has ever existed in the above list. And those who uphold such views will tend to be dismissed as relativists and reckless postmodernists. In this book, I am not seeking to defend those upholding alternative views. As a social scientist, I detect something of enormous cultural and evolutionary significance. I want to understand it better, and I wish to enter into dialogue with all who share this aspiration, filled with a sense of hope desperately needed in our modern world.

Discernment: A New Horizon

I want this book to be mainly an exercise in multidisciplinary discernment, arising primarily from a Christian context, but not exclusively reserved to Christians. *Discernment* is normally associated with the personal pursuit of meaning, seeking out what God wants the individual person to do in terms of serious decisions related to life and faith. The scriptural notion of "discerning the spirits" (1 Cor 12:4–11; 1 Jn 4:1–6) implies a great deal more than an individual pursuit of the will of God.

In mainline Christianity, discernment continues to be a spiritual art, usually associated with spiritual direction, or charismatic prayer, or adopted by the teaching authority of the church itself. In all these cases, it is assumed that authentic discernment is only possible for those who confess and proclaim Jesus as Lord; otherwise we are likely to be dealing with false or evil spiritual influence.

Such concerns seem to arise from a narrow pneumatology (theology of the Holy Spirit), with the Spirit cast in third place, subject to the Father and Jesus, the hierarchical theism claimed by the church to be the basis of its wisdom and power. For reflective adults of the twenty-first century, this understanding of the Holy Spirit is proving to be too reductionist, patriarchal, and even biblically questionable. The adult asks, "Where does this leave the creative empowering Spirit of Genesis 1:1 who calls forth order and creative potential from the foundational chaos of creation?"

In the present work, I outline what is likely to become a much more credible and persuasive pneumatology (theology of the Holy Spirit) for wise elders of the twenty-first century. It is an attempt to retrieve the largely suppressed wisdom of indigenous peoples all over the contemporary world who share a broadly similar belief in the Great Spirit, a subject I explore at length in a previous work (O'Murchu 2012) and summarize in Chapter 3 of the present book.

This ancient, expansive view of the Holy Spirit takes discernment to a whole new level. We are called to attend to the urgings of the Spirit not merely in the human heart (mind and spirit) but as the energizing, empowering source of everything at work in God's creation (cf. Liebert 2015, 21). According to this understanding, humans cannot perceive or comprehend the urgings of the Spirit in the human sphere without first being able to discern how the Spirit works in the entire creation. This is not an undertaking that any one person can pursue on one's own; it will always need to be a collective process, and ideally will need to involve the nonhuman world as well as human beings.

By the same token, it will require a multidisciplinary mode of understanding. Simply quoting scripture at length, with little attention to the original cultural and historical context, is unlikely to lead to a fruitful outcome. If we truly strive to honor the fact that the Spirit fills the whole of God's creation, energizing and sustaining all that happens therein, then we need broad wisdom to read intelligently and sensitively how the Spirit embodies spiritual truth in every domain of creation, including the human. In that case, discernment becomes a complex and prolonged process of listening, praying, striving to understand, engaging, researching, dialoguing, culminating in practical outcomes that themselves will need to be continuously reassessed and discerned anew.

Sr. Elizabeth Liebert of San Francisco Theological Seminary is a leading voice in this expansive view of Christian discernment for the twenty-first century, embracing the wisdom of systems theory and the ensuing structural dynamics so integral to the evolutionary thrust of our time (cf. Liebert, 2015, 54ff). Contrary to the robust individualism, attributed by many to the culture of the Enlightenment (1650–1780), but also rooted in ancient Aristotelian philosophy, a new wave of relationality characterizes our time. It is not entirely new. There is much to suggest that this is how we lived on the earth for much of our evolutionary story (outlined in Chapter 5). If we are to translate this new communal awareness into the cultural and spiritual values of our time, then our strategies of discernment need new foundations at the personal, interpersonal, systemic, and planetary dimensions of our lives.

In other words, discernment in our time needs to pay continued attention to context. Of paramount importance is the evolutionary dimension, stretching us beyond our long allegiance to permanence, the static, and the unchanging. We see things differently now: much more organic, fluid, and flexible. To that evolutionary perspective and its significance for the contemporary adult faith seeker, we now turn our attention.

Chapter 2

The Evolutionary Renaming

Before human beings appeared, evolution had brought forth countless diverse creatures, most of them having little or nothing to do with our own existence yet loved by God. Who knows what further significant developments await emergence in the future?

—Elizabeth Johnson

On the whole we are not conscious of evolution; we do not live as creatures in evolution, and we do not act as if our choices can influence the direction of evolution. . . . In my view, evolution is the story, the metanarrative of our age, . . . When the mind can engage reality as a question rather than imposing prefabricated answers on it, then one can participate creatively in evolution.

—Ilia Delio

Old people, or elder citizens, tend to be perceived as inflexible, staid, and rigid in their views and behaviors. Not so the *wise elders* I have in mind as the target audience of this book. They cherish fluidity and flexibility and a quality of faith that allows for growth and change. They are not much attached to rigid

21

doctrines, forever seeking validation from an unchanging past. Instead they favor an evolutionary view, developing over time, and open to a quality of insight and wisdom unknown to former generations.

While many of these elder folks have no formal theological education or religious formation, they are keenly interested in theological developments, often hold progressive viewpoints, and tend to be more at home in theological reflection along the lines of process theology. They detect, and seek to celebrate, the ubiquitous presence of Holy Mystery in our midst, an evolving sense of Incarnation spread across many eons.

Transcending Incarnational Stasis

Yes, the spiritual seekers I have in mind are aware of the fact that in Christian theology Incarnation has one meaning, and only one: God sent his Son, Jesus, to redeem flawed humanity from sin so that people could obtain salvation in a world hereafter. So, first, let us identify what is being rejected, or more accurately what sense of Incarnation the faith seekers of our time wish to re-vision.

No longer can they accept that the only authentic embodiment of God in our midst happened in and through the historical Jesus, nor can they accept that Jesus is the one and only person who has ever had the experience of being incarnated. From that foundational understanding contemporary faith seekers detect a Christian culture addicted to superiority, arrogance, and exclusivity. Jesus is the only way; no other deified figure holds the same status, and none ever will. Truth is a fixed, unchanging reality and, therefore, totally at variance with any notion of evolutionary development.

To highlight the uniqueness of this one and only Jesus, the inherited Christian story knows no limits to the accolades of power and glory that belong to God's only Son. Like the God-Father who created and rules the world, Jesus is omnipotent (all

powerful), omniscient (all knowing), and beyond human limitation of any type—as in this recent definition of God by a contemporary scientist: "a superhuman, supernatural intelligence
who deliberately designed and created the universe and everything in it, including us." The person who penned these words is
none other than the infamous Richard Dawkins, in his bestsell-
ing book, *The God Delusion* (Dawkins 2006, 31). Dawkins is
a self-avowed atheist, yet thousands of conventional Christian
theologians concur with his definition of God. And that really
baffles the wise elders of our time.

Dawkins claims to be an evolutionist out and out, but obviously there is a huge disconnect between his evolutionary theory
and his theology. Clearly his understanding of theology has not
evolved. He seems to be caught in a time warp, more accurately
a metaphysical warp, that can only envisage God as an exalted
heroic figurehead, beyond time and space. Such an exalted
status translates into a male, patriarchal, royal figurehead, to
which Christians owe absolute submission and obedience. And
bizarrely, it seems that Dawkins also believes in such ideological
submission, creating a penchant of disastrous science as well as
a seriously distorted theology.[1]

This Supreme Being is also human, an attribution that
caused no end of controversy and debate, particularly in the
fourth century, and specifically in the church Councils of Nicea
and Chalcedon. Although the human and the divine are meant
to be equal in the life of the historical Jesus, the divinity is the
trump card, with an unambiguous priority—till the latter half

---

[1] Several reputable scientists identify with this atheistic stance, and in
most cases it arises from an adoption of a static metaphysical understanding of God, which is rapidly losing its meaning and relevance particularly
for adult believers in the twenty-first century. Despite their intelligence and
expertise, such scientists identify with what they think can be the one and
only understanding of God, namely, the inherited patriarchal divine ruler.
Strictly speaking, therefore, lack of faith is not their problem; bankrupt
theology is the problem.

of the twentieth century when Christology (the study of Jesus as the Christ) embraced a range of new insights from other forms of wisdom, notably the social sciences, ancient history, archaeology, etc. Increasingly, it is the *humanity* of Jesus rather than the *divinity* that engages the Christian discernment of the twenty-first century.

When God and Jesus are adorned with metaphysical, patriarchal qualities, inevitably Christian believers become ensnared in codependent relations wherein adulthood is compromised and undermined. All the major religions advocate childlike dependence, which all too often morphs into childish subservience. Codependency has several meanings, but for the present work, it denotes *those collusive behaviors whereby a person ends up behaving like a passive child, thus undermining the evolution of adult maturity.* All the religions liberally encourage their devotees to be obedient servants of childlike disposition. Don't rock the boat, don't ask awkward questions! Remember, in judgment God will judge favorably those who obey. This is the dysfunctionality wise elders seek to outgrow and overcome.

As in several other fields, the evolutionary stretching of knowledge and wisdom—particularly among wise elders, also impacts upon theology, scripture, and, in the case of the present work, on Christology. The shift of emphasis that seeks to view Jesus as the human face of God made radically visible on earth is not so much a denial of divinity as a deepening of what the divine might actually mean. And a second major shift is of a contextual nature: a desire to transcend the anthropocentric metaphysics of early Christian times and replace it with a more organic evolutionary understanding of what it means to be human (as explained in Chapter 5). Finally, we engage the evolutionary shift toward deeper integration, beyond the long-cherished dualistic splitting (human v. human, nature v. grace, body v. spirit, etc.), moving our discernment toward a celebration and affirmation of what binds us together in the one web of universal life.

What Is Evolution About?

Only in the closing decades of the twentieth century did evolution and religion begin to mix. To one degree or another, all the religions convey the sense of a God who does not change and remains steadfast, the same yesterday, today, and forever. And by implication, authentic religion cannot change either; truth is unalterable. Today rapidly growing numbers of people no longer hold these views and are no longer drawn to a religion of fixity and rigid doctrinal truths. Evolution has entered even religious discourse, and evolution denotes change, fluidity, and flexibility. To begin with, I will briefly indicate what I mean by *an evolutionary perspective*, highlighting the following characteristics that are central to the exploration of this book.

- *Aliveness.* Over the past twenty years, our understanding of aliveness has changed dramatically. The propensity for aliveness is no longer reserved to the human, deemed to be superior to all other life-forms. On the contrary, we know that everything that constitutes our embodiment as earthlings is given to us from earth itself, as a living organism, itself energized from the larger cosmic web of life. In theological terms, it is the Holy Spirit who enlivens all that exists (cf. Boff 2015; Haughey 2015). In this context, Incarnation cannot be reserved to one outstanding human-like divine figure; the primary Incarnation of the Holy One in our midst is in creation itself. Much more controversial, and quite new in theological discourse, is our evolving understanding of the Holy Spirit, the One that has traditionally been relegated to a third place, dependent on Father (Creator) and Son (Redeemer) having first done their work, but increasingly being understood as the one who energizes all forms of aliveness (everything in creation), even what we attribute to the Father and Son (see Chapter 3).

- *Emergence.* The all-embracing sense of aliveness unfolds along an evolutionary trajectory that transcends simple cause and effect, with a sense of direction that is open and unpredictable, always evolving into greater complexity (for further elaboration, see Stewart 2000; Delio 2015). The culture of patriarchal certainty, and hierarchical ordering (including that of the doctrine of the Trinity), is increasingly understood as an anthropocentric projection that alienates humans precisely by separating us from the womb of our becoming and attributing to us an elevated status increasingly viewed as exploitative and dangerous. We have ended up with a perverted anthropology, which has seriously distorted how we perceive and understand the humanity of Jesus, with consequent deviations in how we understand the notion of Incarnation.

- *Paradox.* Creation's evolutionary unfolding is endowed with the paradoxical interplay of creation-cum-destruction, an unceasing cyclic rhythm of birth–death–rebirth. Major religions tend to dismiss this paradox as a fundamental flaw requiring divine salvific intervention, particularly through the death and Resurrection of the historical Jesus. A deeper appreciation of this enduring paradox (cf. Chapter 7) alters significantly our understanding of suffering in the world. In the future, our commitment must be one of getting rid of all meaningless suffering, facilitated through a more forthright commitment to peace, justice, and the integrity of God's creation. And this challenge expands the incarnational landscape far beyond the narrow anthropocentric context of conventional Christianity.

- *Lateral Thinking.* Much of Christian theology, and the ensuing spirituality, is defined and described in terms of classical Greek metaphysics, rational thought, and logical argument. It is a linear, sequential process favored by dominant males seeking control and mastery through rational discourse. It is a strategy alien to evolutionary unfolding, lacking in the creativity, imagination, and intuition necessary to apprehend the complexities of this age and every other. Beyond the traditional affiliation with scholastic philosophy, theology must now embrace a multidisciplinary dynamic to engage the lateral consciousness of the twenty-first century, that expansive quality of awareness so typical of the wise elders.

- *Consciousness.* The metaphysical worldview also favored the philosophy of divide and conquer, thus segmenting wisdom and knowledge into binary opposites (dualisms) and uniform categories, alien to the multidisciplinary and transdisciplinary philosophy of our age. According to this latter view, a multidisciplinary perspective is necessary to comprehend the complex mysterious nature of all living reality. Consequently, scripture scholars, in particular, are increasingly adopting a multidisciplinary orientation in their research and discernment, embracing a range of social sciences as well as the wisdom of ancient history and the corroborative evidence of archaeological discoveries; for the theological implications, see Kelly (2015). Contrary to the fear of several fundamentalists, such a broad interdisciplinary base—a new quality of consciousness—does not diminish the truth of faith but for a growing body of adult faith seekers enriches and deepens their spirituality.

- *Spirituality.* All over the contemporary world, mainline religion is in recession (with the possible exception of Islam), yielding pride of place either to more amorphous spiritual offshoots or to violent ideologies that will eventually destroy the very religion they seek to safeguard and promote. Nearly all formal religious traditions embody imperial sentiment, a derogatory view of creation, and a distinctly male, patriarchal bias.

An alternative spiritual hunger has surfaced (and has been suppressed) many times in the history of the great religions; it sometimes morphs into a phenomenon known as mysticism, which enjoys a distinctive revival in recent decades (cf. Johnson and Ord 2012). Under this novel spiritual development, Incarnation takes on an expansive meaning beyond its conventional Christian significance.

- *Cooperation.* From a human perspective, evolution is not solely dependent on the survival of the fittest, but rather on the triumph of cooperation. For John Stewart (2000) cooperation is evolution's arrow: "Cooperators will inherit the earth, and eventually the universe" (Stewart 2000, 8). However, it has to be a quality of cooperation that can embrace and integrate legitimate self-interest. This is the kind of integration that wise elders desire. And it is remarkably similar to the supreme goal of both Judaism and Christianity: Love God! And to do that, one has to love the neighbor, which is only genuinely possible when we learn to love ourselves (cf. Lv 19:18; Mk 12:29–30). Genuine self-interest is not contrary to faith in God, or to faith in evolution; it is the prerequisite for both.

- *Discernment.* As already indicated in Chapter 1, Christian discernment describes the human effort to discover, appropriate, and integrate God's desires for our growth and development as people of faith. In its popular (Ignatian) sense, it is very much an individual process between the person and God, with the spiritual director acting as a guide or facilitator. Group discernment is a more loosely defined process often invoked at religious gatherings and in areas of pastoral accountability (see Liebert 2015). In the ecclesiastical context, discernment is understood to be the divinely bestowed prerogative of the teaching authority of the church—to which all other forms of discernment need to be accountable. In a world and church becoming increasingly suspicious of the integrity and truth of institutional guidance, the task of discernment for the future will become much more localized, dialogically mediated, and informed by the skills and wisdom of systems theory (in other words, multidisciplinary). Increasingly, personal and group discernment will interweave, with wisdom from the ground up, commanding much stronger credibility than that which comes from the top down. Theological and scriptural insight will no longer be seen as a reserve of the academic scholar, but rather a dialogical process, reclaiming and reviving the often neglected notion of the *sensus fidelium*.

Our evolutionary propensities mark a seismic shift from a worldview in which we were "captivated by the spell of solidity, the fallacy of fixity, the illusion of immobility, the semblance of stasis, but the evolution revolution is starting to break that spell. We are realizing that we are, in fact, not standing on solid ground. But neither are we adrift in a meaningless universe. . . . We are part and parcel of a vast process of becoming." (Phipps 2012, 26). Phipps (2012, 32) goes on to identify three characteristics common to evolutionary thinkers (and to the wise elders) of the twenty-first century:

- Evolutionaries are cross-disciplinary generalists.
- They develop the capacity to cognize the vast timescales of our evolutionary history.
- They embody a new spirit of optimism.

And this spirit of optimism is one important dimension of the spiritual convergence characterizing our time. Sometimes, scientists are ahead of religionists in viewing a spiritual way forward: "In recent years there has been a resurgence of interest in the connections that might serve to reunify the scientific world-view with the religious instinct. Much of the discussion is tentative, and the difficulties in finding an accommodation remain daunting, but it is more than worth the effort. In my opinion, it will be our lifeline" (Conway Morris 2003, 328).

Jesus in an Evolutionary Context

Throughout this book, I embrace an evolutionary imperative, supporting the view that *evolution is central to our understanding of life at every level.* Volumes have been written on evolution, and much of it is narrowly and ideologically defined in neo-Darwinian terms. For the present work, I wish to transcend much of the sophisticated rhetoric and get straight to the core elements of *growth–change–development.* These three words captivate the deep truth of what we mean by evolution but also the core dynamics of incarnational development:

- Everything within and around us *grows*; that seems an indisputable fact of the natural and human worlds.
- We perceive *change* all around us, and this involves decline and death. Such disintegration is not an evil, nor is it the consequence of sin (cf. Rom 6:23), but a God-given dimension of all creation.
- I also adopt a key insight of the philosopher Karl Popper, and articulated anew by the contemporary theologian John F. Haught (2010, 2015), that the direction of evolution takes shape primarily in response to *the lure of the future* and not merely solidifying what has served us well in the past. In the words of John Haught (2015, 52): "Evolution, viewed theologically, means that creation is still happening and that God is creating and saving the world not *a retro*, that is, by pushing it forward out of the past, but *ab ante*, by calling it from up ahead." Theologically, I understand that the central attraction of the lure of the future is a fruit and wisdom of the Holy Spirit.

Now we come to a critical question that, undoubtedly, readers will have already raised: Are we trying to force Jesus (and our Christian faith) into yet another cultural ghetto, or does the authentic Jesus—historically and Christologically—belong to an evolutionary context, which conventional Christian scholarship has long ignored, or underestimated? Can Jesus be re-visioned within the evolutionary process of growth–change–development instead of the time frame of Greek metaphysics and other cultural impositions from a past that largely resists change and growth? And while Christian scholarship tends to judge truth and authenticity by fidelity to an unchanging and unchangeable past, might it be possible that Jesus represents for Christians an open-ended future forever awaiting fuller realization?

In the mid-twentieth century, Christian faith began to embrace new evolutionary thresholds that would destabilize the imperial monolithic monopoly of several previous centuries. Three events are worthy of note. First is the demythologization of scripture advocated by German Lutheran theologian Rudolf Bultmann (d.1976) outlined in his essay *New Testament and Mythology* (1941) and in his *Kerygma and Myth*, originally published in German in 1948. Second is the discovery of the Nag Hammadi collection of Gnostic texts in Upper Egypt in 1945, including the *Gospel of Thomas*, documents that highlight another strand of Christian wisdom long suppressed in previous centuries (cf. Patterson 2014). Third is a grossly underestimated development in twentieth-century Catholicism, the publication of *Divino Afflante Spiritu* (on the most opportune way to promote biblical studies) by Pope Pius XII in 1943, calling for translations of the Bible from original languages and not merely from the Latin Vulgate; this document was hailed by the late Raymond Brown as a Magna Carta for biblical progress.

In 1977, British New Testament scholar James G. D. Dunn published his *Unity and Diversity in the New Testament*, highlighting the complex range of understandings that prevailed in early Christian times on almost every aspect of faith. Such acknowledgment of diversity and pluriformity is now viewed as a necessary and healthy dimension of all evolutionary growth. It challenges several long-held views on the meaning of Jesus and of Christian faith, throwing up a range of new questions on the meaning of Incarnation—historically and for the twenty-first century.

For spiritual seekers of the twenty-first century, these are questions for daily conversation and integral to the search for deeper truth in the contemporary world. In addressing these questions, I am adopting a number of insights that have been central to the evolving Christology of late twentieth and early twenty-first centuries:

- The time frame associated with the historical Jesus—the axial context of two thousand years ago—must be contextualized anew within the evolving understanding of the creation we inhabit, particularly the enlarged chronology of planet earth and the vast time spans within which we know the universe today.[2] As indicated in Genesis 1:1, the creative Spirit of God has been fully at work since the dawn of creation (cf. Edwards 2004, 1), and if we are to view Jesus as a Spirit-filled person (suggested by the late Marcus Borg, among many others), we must transcend the two thousand year benchmark that we have often literalized in a dangerously ideological way. This is not merely another attempt at reconciling the Christ of faith (the cosmic Christ) with the historical Jesus. Rather

---

[2] I am aware of the fact that a growing body of cosmologists wish to extend our acquaintance with universal life beyond the one-cycle universe to the vaster and more complex possibility of a *multiverse,* and personally I feel strongly attracted to that possibility. However, for the purposes of the present book, I will remain within the conventional time span of a universe that began to evolve about 13.7 billion years ago, and is predicted to continue unfolding for at least another ten billion years. For readers interested in the notion of a multiverse, see Rubenstein (2014) and one of several attempts to explore the theological implications in Kraay (2014).

the task at hand is to highlight the archetypal significance of the historical Jesus, not merely for Christians but for people of all times and cultures (see Chapter 5).

- Traditionally, Incarnation has been viewed as a human endowment, largely if not totally reserved to human beings. As indicated in Chapter 1, theologians today opt for a broader understanding—with archetypal over-tones—that Incarnation denotes *embodiment*. That all forms of embodiment—from bacteria to the universe—evidences a God who loves bodies and chooses the cor-poreal form in every initiative of cocreation. Everything in creation grows and flourishes in an embodied con-text. While spirit represents the energetic life force of everything in creation, clearly the body is the medium through which Spirit power evolves and flourishes. How do we reconceptualize Incarnation to include all forms of embodiment from the cosmos itself to the tiny bacte-ria, and how do we re-vision the embodiment of Jesus as a fresh and empowering articulation of that vision? I will deal with that complex challenge in Chapter 4.

- By realigning our understanding of Incarnation with this more expansive approach to embodiment, we need to reconsider what it means to be human within a revamped Christology. The anthropological context needs substantial attention and discernment. If Jesus represents a new breakthrough for the human species, traditionally described in terms of salvation and redemp-tion, why reduce it to a mere two thousand years ago, when humanity has flourished over a time span of *sev-eral million years*? And why do we associate Jesus so exclusively with the negative, sinful side, when our long evolutionary story illuminates so many other capacities? I deal with this question in Chapter 5.

- Next is the cultural context, within which I will high-light merely one crucial factor: *imperial kingship*. It seems to me that Christian scholars have not dealt well with this substantial background material, with some notable exceptions, specifically the American scripture scholar Wes Howard-Brook (2010, 2016). In the time of Jesus, God was understood to be a king-like figure who reigned in the heavens above and ruled all on earth through a hierarchical set of structures. It was inconceivable that such a God would send the divine rescuer in any other manner other than as a king-like savior. As a growing body of postcolonial scholars indicate, this ideological allegiance to the kingship of Jesus—historically reinforced mainly through Roman Emperor Constantine—has been Christianity's greatest liability (see O'Murchu 2014a). As I shall indicate in Chapter 6, it is the primary area that needs substantial redress, as we seek to unravel and rectify the several imperial and violent projections attributed to both God and Jesus down through the ages.

- There is a spiritual dimension that has been largely overlooked throughout the past two thousand years. Scholars throughout the twentieth century have been at pains to reclaim and integrate afresh the *Jewishness* of Jesus. Certainly, there has been an anti-Semitic rhetoric around Jesus that needs to be addressed (and dispensed with), but in the process of doing so, Jesus is reinstated as an adherent of a formal religion, a strategy that may be more a projection of religious devotees themselves rather than a genuine discernment on what Jesus actually represents. If we prioritize the New Reign of God as recommended in the gospels (cf. Matt 6:33), then we have to wrestle with the fact that Jesus seems to be on to something bigger and broader than any formal religion, Judaism included. Purists will try to argue—as they do in every religion—that the largest and deepest vision that Jesus could possibly have employed is already there in the Hebrew scriptures and that Christianity merely makes it more explicit. In the present work, I follow the line adopted by many social scientists who view each religion as culturally and historically conditioned, while *spirituality* is much more generic, deeper, and expansive. More than anything else, what I am pursuing in the present work is a spirituality of the gospels, transcending the several religious ideologies accumulated over the centuries, and illuminating afresh in the radical creativity of Jesus—and of several other spiritual illuminaries—with incarnational consequences of cosmic and planetary significance.

- So, Christian discipleship today is evolving, beyond the admiration for, and worship of, a divine patriarchal hero, into a collaborative endeavor for empowering love and justice, fired by the radical vision of the New Reign of God, renamed in this book as *the Companionship of Empowerment*, with the historical Jesus as the exemplary disciple and all others (Christians and others) called into codiscipleship in that enterprise. As an undertaking, it knows no boundaries: ethnic, cultural, or religious! It is a global enterprise embracing all that is holy and sacred within the entire web of life, cosmic and planetary alike. That is what contemporary visionaries— like the wise elders—know as *incarnational wholeness*.

Revelation: The Expanded View

In the midst of this evolutionary movement, the devoted religionist is likely to query the truth upon which I base my claims, and will wonder what has happened to the notion of *divine revelation* and its guarantee of reliable truth from the wellspring of divine wisdom (the deposit of faith). The notion of revelation is a lynchpin of Christian theology. It may be defined as *the communication of some truth by God to a rational creature*

through means that are beyond the ordinary course of nature.
For fundamental Christians, and also for Muslims, Sikhs, and
some Hindus, revelation denotes words spoken by God to an
inspired recipient who then reproduces the words as faithfully
as possible. For instance, Muslims believe that the Quran was
revealed by God to Muhammad—word by word—through the
angel Gabriel.

Christians tend not to make claims as explicit as that.
Instead, they invoke the notion of *inspiration*, involving a special
illumination of the mind, in virtue of which the recipient con-
ceives such thoughts as God desires him/her to commit to writing, a process that does not necessarily involve supernatural communication (in the direct sense). According to Christianity, God
took the initiative of self-revelation. The story of this initiative is
presented in the inspired writing of the Bible, where God speaks
in human languages that are intelligible and capable of being
understood throughout the ages. Revelation does not diminish
human empirical abilities of knowledge but unveils facts that are
beyond these abilities.

Revelation also denotes a quality of divine illumination,
something previously hidden, that has now been made visible (in
and through Jesus) and *never before* accessible to human beings.
In other words, this teaching seems to assume that revelation
is only possible through human beings, and since humans have
always been in the dark—in the grip of a fundamental corruption
(e.g., Original Sin)—the revelation is only possible through special intervention by God, with a view to rescuing and redeeming
flawed humanity. Consequently, there seems to be no possibility of creation itself enhancing or enriching our understanding
of revelation. The underlying, unexamined logic seems to be, if
humans are flawed, everything in creation must be flawed as
well. This dangerously ideological view of humanity seems to
be the cul-de-sac that has led several religions into dead ends.
It effectively undermines all attempts at a more coherent and
responsible understanding of Incarnation.

The great champion of Catholic thought, Thomas Aquinas, believed in two types of revelation from God, *general revelation* and *special revelation*. In general revelation, God reveals the Godself through creation itself such that at least some truths about God can be learned by the empirical study of nature, through physics, cosmology, and other sciences. Special revelation is the knowledge of God and spiritual matters obtained by an individual through supernatural means such as visions, mystical states, speaking in tongues, charismatically inspired intuitions.

Though one may deduce the existence of God and some of God's attributes through general revelation, certain specifics may be known only through special revelation. Aquinas believed that special revelation is equivalent to how God is made manifest in the life and ministry of Jesus, necessary for salvation, and carrying a form of divine wisdom that uniquely supersedes the revealed truth of all other religions. Moreover, it can only be authentically received and interpreted by those specifically called forth to do so, namely, the church's teaching authority. Thus, we arrive at the point where authentic revealed truth belongs primarily, if not exclusively, to Christianity.

The complex nature of this topic can be gleaned from an oft-cited Catholic source, namely, Avery Dulles's *Models of Revelation* (1983), in which the late Jesuit scholar outlines five possible models: revelation as doctrine, as history, as inner experience, as dialectical encounter, as new awareness. When this book was first published, it was the last two models that were considered as breaking new ground. *Dialectical encounter* basically suggests that the more we come to know God, the more we realize how little we do know, and *the new awareness* suggests that our understanding of revelation will expand and deepen as knowledge advances.

This brings me to the view gradually gaining acceptance in the twenty-first century: The mystery and reality of God is manifest (or revealed) to us *primarily in God's creation*, in a process that has been unfolding over several millennia—and will continue to evolve into the open-ended future. Each religion might be considered a specific attempt to appropriate that revelation for a particular cultural ethos and from within a specific historical context. Fundamentalists will dismiss that view as relativism; for them, God can only reveal Godself in absolutes, and each group claims that its absolutes are true while all others are false (to varying degrees). It does not take too much insight to realize that colonial power games are at work here, with remnants of patriarchal domination and Greek rationality dictating our understanding of truth.[3]

Throughout the present work, I embrace the cosmic and planetary dimensions as the primary context for divine revelation. In other words, *God has been fully manifesting God's self in the evolutionary unfolding of creation through many eons.* Long before humans evolved (an estimated seven million years ago), and long before formal religion or churches ever came to be, God's gracious and empowering creativity inundated every fiber of the cosmic creation. Nor was that effusively dynamic divine life force looking down the time line to a time capsule of two thousand years ago when the evolutionary process would have to undergo a major redemptive realignment because this magnificently creative force somehow made a major blunder along the way. The divine creative imperative is a resounding "Yes" to all that can become—and to paraphrase St. Paul, when God says, "Yes" that affirmation is never compromised. (2 Cor 1:19–20).

---

[3] It is worth noting in passing that the Christian doctrine of revelation was drawn up in early Christian times by a small elite group of European (Roman) males, with no input from females, or the rest of humanity. Nor was any consideration given to how the other creatures inhabiting creation might contribute to our understanding of revelation. Contemporary adults find it impossible to believe in a God who could be so imperially selective and so anthropocentrically exclusive.

Proactive Christianity

Thanks to the evolutionary wisdom of our time, and related factors such as the information explosion, multiculturalism, insight from multidisciplinary research, and egalitarian collaboration, any claim to exclusivity will evoke suspicion and will fail to deliver a deeper sense of truth, particularly for the wise elders of our time. Of course, this major cultural shift also begets a range of defensive allegations, focused on postmodern fluidity, rabid individualism, hedonism, and moral relativism. These are certainly troubling trends that require discerning redress; unfortunately, the major religions seem largely unable to offer informed and empowering responses, which leaves us with a cultural vacuum not likely to be evacuated for quite a long time.

It is precisely from within this cultural vacuum that I raise many of the pressing questions that this book seeks to address, particularly what a resilient humanity might look like in the twenty-first century and what is spiritually required to sustain and advance it. It is becoming unquestionably clear that it has to be a way of being human that is deeply integrated within the planetary and cosmic wisdom coming to the fore in our age. It is a journey toward a deeper integration, requiring an ever more amorphous, multidisciplinary process. And paradoxically, it begets the inevitable questions of meaning and spiritual purpose at a time when many adult faith seekers are reluctant to look to formal religion for resolution or discerning guidelines for the future.

I believe that a revamped sense of Christian faith has a substantial contribution to make to this endeavor, and it needs to be one that seeks to recapture a long-neglected foundational belief in the New Reign of God, described in the gospels as the Kingdom of God. It is the translation of that ideal into lived reality that constitutes the task of incarnational becoming as explored in the pages of this book.

Incarnation did not begin with the divine deliverance of our Christian faith. Divine rescue is not the primary purpose of our Christian faith. Rather than marking the beginning of human salvation, Christianity can be understood as a high point in a divine initiative that goes back over many millennia. It is not an exclusive Christian claim; we discern parallels in all the great world religions (cf. O'Murchu 2008, 144–49). The narrow reductionism of the formal Christian era is increasingly seen as a dangerous, myopic, a sectarian dead end. It is much more about human imperialism than the liberating power of divine grace.

As a Christian term, *grace* denotes graciousness, giftedness, and generosity. It describes the divine initiative, usually light years ahead of our human imaginations. It opens up the mystery within which we live, and move, and have our being. From within that spacious, grace-filled landscape, we embrace the task of this book: to illuminate afresh God's gracious embodiment in the midst of creation. The challenge is captivated in these inspiring words of the ethicist Margaret A. Farley (2008, 117):

> We live incarnated in a world that is revelatory of the sacred. We are gifted in body and spirit by all creation's speaking to us God's word and providing for us a home where we can find sustenance and joy. We embody ourselves in intimate relationships with one another, and in less intimate though still bodily relationships with many others in societies where our dwellings extend our skins and we learn to thirst not only in body but in spirit. We are the ones who ask questions of ourselves as embodied and who can encounter God in whatever searches we undertake and whatever answers we find. . . . I will also propose that the self-transcendence that Christians associate with what it means to be a human person pertains to ourselves not just as spirits but as bodies.

In the present work, I bring together the wisdom of the social sciences, with more recent theological insight, to reexamine the notion of *Incarnation*. The God who befriends us in our human embodiment has been journeying with us for a long time, an evolutionary trajectory outstripping the more than two thousand years postulated by Christianity. As a human species, we have known Immanuel—God is with us—for several thousands of years. That Immanuel however did not first appear in the historical Jesus of more than two thousand years ago. That energizing incarnational presence had been around for billions of years previously. We now encounter the foundational incarnating creativity, known for several centuries as the *Great Spirit*, the topic to which we now turn our discerning attention.

Chapter 3

In the Beginning Was the Spirit

The Spirit's presence and activity are universal, limited neither by space nor time.

—Pope John Paul II

Neglect of the Spirit and the religious value of the natural world seem to go hand in hand.

—Elizabeth Johnson

Humans have long speculated on the origins of religious belief and have come up with a variety of explanations, chief among them being the experience of *animism*. Basically it means that everything is endowed with a soul, an inner sense of aliveness that in time came to be named as God. Animism is generally perceived as an ancient, primitive belief and practice, based on the infantile projections of an ignorant, prerational people.

Obviously, this is an explanation conjured up by people who saw themselves as more advanced, rationally minded, and representing the superior status of male hegemony.[1] They also tend

---

[1] Celia Deane-Drummond (2014, 82, 143) of Notre Dame University (United States), commenting on the inherited influence of both Aristotle and

to take the world's formal religions as normative—primarily if not exclusively for human persons, and not merely for contemporary peoples but for anybody that has ever lived. And among the formal religions, Westerners tend to favor the monotheistic faiths of Judaism, Christianity, and Islam as being more advanced and authentic.

The favored regard for monotheistic religion carries patriarchal preoccupations that frequently go unchecked and remain largely unexamined. In these faiths, Incarnation is understood as an ideal embodiment of God on earth, made possible in and through an ideal male, which, in turn, translates into one of royal lineage. This preoccupation is clearly visible in Christianity in the opening chapter of Matthew's Gospel, in which Jesus's ancestry is traced back to Abraham. Luke (Chapter 3) embellishes the genealogy even further by tracing Jesus back to Adam.

Such is the preoccupation with the divine presence in the world, viewed from within formal religion generally and specifically from within monotheistic faiths, that we have largely lost sight of how the divine infiltrates and informs the rest of creation. In fact, all formal religion, to one degree or another, regards the material creation as inimical to religious faith; seeking the divine in the natural world has frequently been condemned as pantheism or idolatry.

There are notable exceptions. First is the growing body of data (based on scholarly research) of how our ancient ancestors felt and experienced the sacredness of life all around them. We detect this religious sentiment in ancient art and architecture, in ritual behavior dating back several thousands of years (an estimated seventy thousand years in the case of ritualized burials), and in the much

---

Thomas Aquinas, makes this astute observation: "Overall, the work of grace is primarily directed towards the reasoning process in Aquinas' scheme, so that four of the seven gifts of the Spirit are connected to reason, namely, wisdom, knowledge, understanding, counsel—the other three to appetite: fortitude, piety, and fear. . . . For Aristotle, the rational soul belongs to the nonsexual aspect of the human; however, in the case of the male something of the soul can also be detected in the life-giving power of the male semen."

disputed worship centered around the Great Mother Goddess of Paleolithic times (cf. Reid-Bowen 2007). For contemporary adult faith seekers, these are reservoirs of an ancient and enduring wisdom that merit a more benign discernment.

Our tendency to judge all religious behavior from within the sphere of formal religion leaves us with a functionalist view of religion incapable of embracing a deeper, older, and much more dynamic view of the sacred in our midst. Our anthropocentric preoccupation (placing humans first) seriously undermines and distorts the breadth and depth of religious sentiment. There is a great deal more to transcendent faith than what concerns humans as human. It is not just about humans but very much about the planetary and cosmic contexts in which humans evolve, grow, and develop. Long before we came on the scene as a new earthly species, holiness flourished. Our perceptual horizon has been too narrow. The time has come to explore its enlarged horizons.

Enter the Great Spirit

This is a book about Incarnation, which, for the moment, I understand to mean *God's embodiment in creation as experienced and named by human beings.* The oldest and most enduring articulations of such experience are captivated in what indigenous peoples all over our world describe as the *Great Spirit.* Many of these contemporary peoples have never had direct contact or communication with each other, yet they all uphold a very similar set of religious convictions, centered on the notion of the Great Spirit.

For purposes of the present work, I'll offer a brief overview of how these peoples understand the Great Spirit; for further elaboration, see my book, *In the Beginning Was the Spirit* (O'Murchu 2012). While most mainline religions define God as transcendent Spirit (a disembodied reality beyond time and space, yet impacting intimately through time and space as pure spirit), the notion of the Great Spirit seeks to describe God's intimate and enduring presence to all organic life *primarily in and through the material creation itself.* It is through our cosmic interaction *as earthlings* that we encounter and experience the Great Spirit.

Christianity postulates a male progenitor, the Father, as the oldest identity of the divine in our midst, but according to the world's indigenous peoples, it is the Holy Spirit and not the Father who comes first. Contemporary theological discernment seems to be moving in that direction. According to the theologian Leonardo Boff, "What came 'before the before' is what theology calls *Spiritus Creator,* the Creative Spirit" (Boff 2015,160), which Boff goes on to flesh out in these words:

> The first divine person to come into this world, to break into the evolutionary process, was not the Word, or the Son, but the Holy Spirit. The third person in the order of the Trinity comes first in the order of creation. . . . something about human beings refuses to think of things as simply scattered about, thrown together any such way. They see an organizing principle that brings things together to form a cosmos instead of chaos. They sense that a powerful and loving Energy is in action, upholding, preserving, and moving things forward together. They dare to give a name to this mysterious and fascinating reality. They give it names inspired by veneration and respect. What is more they can enter into dialogue with it, celebrate it with rituals, dance, and feasts. They feel it as an inner enthusiasm (from the Greek word for "God" within). It inspires feelings of reverence, devotion, and worship. (Boff 2015, 120, 135)

Another contemporary theologian, John C. Haughey (2015, 69) adds this observation: "The Spirit has been accompanying the workings of nature in the entire course of its evolution." Instead of dismissing ancient wisdom as primitive and infantile, Boff avers that something much more profound and enduring has been at work. The oldest human intuition into the meaning of the divine was intimately and integrally experienced within our convivial relationship with creation itself. This is an ancient *theodicy* with a profound meaning we have scarcely begun to discern. And for the present work, I am suggesting it is the oldest and deepest understanding of Incarnation known to humans.

According to the belief in the Great Spirit, God's primordial Incarnation is *not in the human but in the cosmic creation.* Even a secular voice, that of the physicist Hans-Peter Durr, endorses this view: "I have spent fifty years—my entire life as a researcher—to ask, what is it that hides behind the material. And the result is simple: there is no matter! Basically, there is only spirit" (quoted in Schafer 2013, 19).

Everything born out of that creation—including humans—mirrors the divine presence, and especially its potential for cocreativity. Energy is the primary stuff through which the Spirit operates. While physics hesitates to explore the meaning of energy—what energizes the energy itself—First Nations peoples know intuitively what the answer is, a resonance congruent with the wisdom of adult faith seekers today. And while science tends to view energy as functional and random (till we humans choose to do something with it), faith in the Great Spirit clearly asserts that the primary energizer, the creator and sustainer of all that is, is none other than the Great Spirit.

Several crucial issues arise here, all bordering on the heretical as far as formal religion is concerned. First, the energy itself is not some mysterious illusive force entering the world from some distant heavenly realm or irrupting for the first time in the Big Bang. It is integral to the unfolding of creation from the *beginning*, which as modern science intimates should be thought of as *infinity:* a multiuniverse without beginning or end.

Second, while accepting the Darwinian dynamic of chance and necessity, even some scientists acknowledge that there is within creation a preferred sense of direction (e.g., Gould 1994; Stewart 2000; Conway Morris 2003), which Teilhard de Chardin described as growth into greater complexity.

Third, the life force behind and within this energizing force is not a personal God as understood by formal religion. But neither is it impersonal, the binary opposite to our notion of the personal. We could describe it as *transpersonal*, embracing all that impacts upon the human but forever seeking the fuller integration of the human into the planetary and cosmic web of life. The anthropology that arises here will be further explored later in this book.

Fourth, the creative life force, described in Christianity as the Father, is itself energized by the Great Spirit. Therefore, the descending order of Father, Son, and Holy Spirit, so widely taken for granted in Christianity, with parallels in some of the other great religions, is unknown in the faith of First Nations peoples. For First Nations spirituality, the Spirit comes *first*, and all other aspects of revelation, including the Father and Jesus, ensue thereafter. The theological implications have been explored, mainly by Asian scholars such as Peter Phan (2004), Young Lee (1996), and Grace Ji-Sun Kim (2011).

Finally, the notion of a divine rescue so central to the soteriology of the Christian faith has no place in the spirituality of the Great Spirit. The responsibility for overcoming sin and evil is a *human undertaking* facilitated by a more discerning collaboration with the Great Spirit. And in this task, our human regard for the land is foundational. When we learn afresh to befriend the living earth itself, then we will see and understand differently, and learn to behave in a manner more congruent with our earthling-status as spirit-infused creatures. And lest the reader think I have slipped into some kind of new-age utopianism, I will deal later with the paradox of pain, suffering, sin, and evil.

Incarnating Presence

What I am presenting and unraveling in this chapter is the spiritual insight of First Nations peoples all over our world, that God's revelation to us, God's presence with us, and the divine incarnational insertion among us, *belongs, first and foremost, to creation itself.* This is not pantheism in any shape or form. It is a new way—albeit very ancient—of understanding God's participation in our world and requires us to revision afresh our role in that creation.

At this juncture I need to distinguish between creation in its full cosmic scope (what we study in cosmology and quantum physics) and our human experience of that creation always mediated from our earth perspective. In First Nations spirituality, the Great Spirit denotes God's involvement in the entire creation, particularly over the several billennia before planet earth came to be. However, it is in and through our engagement with the earth that humans connect with the workings of the Great Spirit. We experience the Spirit's animation and Incarnation in every aspect of creation, but it is always mediated and reflected in our dealings with the earth. Thus, we begin to appropriate the kind of symbiosis depicted by the American theologian Mark Wallace (2005, 125, 147): "The Spirit ensouls the earth as its life-giving breath, and the earth embodies the Spirit's mysterious interanimation of the whole creation. . . . The world's forests are the lungs we breathe with, the ozone layer is the skin that protects; and the earth's lakes and rivers are the veins and arteries that supply us with vital fluids."

Both aspects are crucial to the expanded understanding of Incarnation explored in the present work. The entire universe is God's primary revelation to us, where the energizing Spirit has been at work for time immemorial. Throughout the twentieth century, our appreciation and understanding of universal life has been stretched considerably thanks to new scientific breakthroughs in relativity, quantum physics, and cosmology; and for wise elders particularly, this scientific knowledge often carries profound spiritual and theological insight.

The late Judy Cannato (2006, 65) captivates the growing sense of mystery that such cosmic engagement awakens in this memorable quote:

The water in your body contains primordial hydrogen formed in the first seconds of the Big Bang. The carbon atoms that formed you came together after the explosion of a supernova. The concentration of salt in your body matches the concentration of salt in the ancient seas. Your cells are direct descendants of unicellular organisms that developed billions of years ago. You see because chlorophyll molecules mutated, so that like plant leaves, your eyes can capture the light from the sun. And in your mother's womb your tiny body repeated the whole process of multi-cellular life on earth, beginning with a single cell, and then developing greater and greater complexity.

In a word, the human body is intimately linked not merely with the earth body but with the cosmic body as well. Incarnationally, our corporeal identity is that of sun-energy, stardust, and the interwoven complexity of several energy forces belonging to the vast womb of our evolving universe. Although this cosmic dimension is of primary importance for a revived sense of our incarnational meaning and integrity, it will not receive extensive coverage in the present work. A vast range of written resources already exist, including Swimme and Berry (1992), Primark and Abrams (2007), Judy Cannato (2006, 2010), Swimme and Tucker (2011). In the present work, I will concentrate on the earthly dimension, our status and integrity as earthlings, and the central place of our earthiness in a revamped understanding of Incarnation.

I prioritize our earthiness, and our sacred significance as earthlings, chiefly because of the prolonged demonization of our earth-dwelling over several centuries, manifested to one degree or another in all the world's major religions. Instead of emphasizing holiness and divine deliverance through escape from this vale of tears to the fulfillment of a distant heaven, the vision I am outlining implies a radical commitment to cocreating heaven on earth. It is in and through our earthiness that we serve God and work out our own salvation and the well-bring of all that has been entrusted to our care.

Amid these reflections three issues in particular require clarification: (1) our understanding of God, (2) creation as fundamentally sacred, and (3) the collaborative endeavor of cocreation. From the human perspective, I begin with the second, namely, *creation*, not with the first. Naturalist, David Abram, states the challenge in vividly forthright terms:

> An eternity we thought was elsewhere now calls out to us from every cleft in every stone, from every cloud and clump of dirt. To lend our ears to the dripping glaciers—to come awake to the voices of silence—is to be turned inside out, discovering to our astonishment that the wholeness and holiness we've been drawing our way toward has been holding us all along; that the secret and sacred One that moves behind all the many traditions is none other than this animate immensity that enfolds us, this spherical eternity, glimpsed at last in its unfathomable wholeness and complexity, in its sensitivity and its sentience. (Abram 2010, 181)

Long before religion ever unfolded in the formal ways we know today, our ancient ancestors engaged with Holy Mystery and appropriated its benevolence through a range of rituals and ensuing ethical behaviors. Central to this spiritual view was a deep intuitive sense of the sacredness of creation itself, energized and sustained by the living Spirit who blew with the wind, warmed with fire-heat, flowed in the water, danced with the animals, and spoke in the vibrations of human sound.

In his book on the Holy Spirit, American theologian, John C. Haughey (2015, 194) makes this pertinent observation:

> Ironically, in this we are becoming more like our forebears, the many early peoples who recognized and worshipped in many different ways *a numinous presence*

in nature. Although a transhuman causality was recognized by our human ancestors from the earliest times as archaeological, anthropological, and historical studies of their practices of worship have unearthed, we moderns might be coming so full of knowledge that we do not see what our forebears saw. . . . The transhuman component could be more easily seen *as Spirit* if there were a willingness on the part of theologians to be engaged with and informed by what the sciences have been learning about every history and matter. (emphasis mine)

For our ancient ancestors, their Emmanuel (God with us) was far more real and tangible than how many Christians today experience the Incarnation of God in our midst. And their nature-based faith was far less amenable to idolatry as later religion came to be. Even to this day, First Nations peoples do not pray to the Great Spirit nor do they worship it. Rather to paraphrase St. Paul (Rom 8:26ff), it is the Spirit who prays in and through the people. The primary purpose of indigenous rituals is not to beseech or pacify the deity but to become more disposed to collaborate responsibly with the Great Spirit.[2]

The rituals help to ground the people in their land, the primary mediating force for the wisdom and energy of the Great Spirit. And the closer the people remain to the natural world, deeply respectful of its rhythms, while in awe and fear, remaining open to the great paradox of creation-cum-destruction, then the people know intimately the God who befriends them in good times and bad, in fortune and misfortune alike. The long history of the human species suggests that when humans remain very close to nature, we tend to do the right things. When we set ourselves over against creation, as we have been progressively doing

---

[2] Admittedly, over time, the rituals have become distorted and even perverted, but this often happened because of the influence of Christian missionaries, and throughout the twentieth century, by Muslim proselytizers, especially in North and West Africa.

since the Agricultural Revolution (about 8,000 BCE), we create the evil that so seriously undermines all sense of meaning in our lives (for more on the development of agriculture, see Chapter 5).

Once we are clear on what a right relationship with God's creation might look like, we can begin to engage the God questions. Many of our prevailing notions about God, elaborated at length in the scriptures of the great religions, are essentially projections of rabid patriarchal conquerors. By pushing God from creation back into heaven, we have engaged in a convoluted double deal:

- We have rid creation of the Holy One so that we can continue unchecked on our brutal game of divide and conquer, the basis of so much exploitative consumerism, and destructive violence in our world.
- We have invented a heavenly monstrosity so brutal that God is prepared to sacrifice Godself's own beloved one to redeem us from the mess we ourselves have created.

So, who or what is this God that the world religions are so enamored about? Is it not precisely the invented projection that F. LeRon Shults (2014) so ingeniously describes in what he labels a *postpartum* theology (as distinct from a postmortem, death-of-God analysis), the God humans gave birth to in order validate and sanction their insatiable desire to conquer and control. Unfortunately, Shults himself gets stuck in the anthropocentric interpretation, lacking that mystical intuition that can see sacredness beyond the human purvey; he also lacks the psychological insight to realize that projections can serve a variety of purposes, some of which are ultrareal and not based on mere delusions.

The God invented by the major religions is born out of a consciousness shift fueled largely by the fear of chaos. The more egalitarian, integral relationship with the earth, which seems to have prevailed for much of the Paleolithic era, came to what seems a rather abrupt end as the ice sheets spread down from

Europe with a devastating impact on what Steve Taylor (2005) calls *Saharasia* (North Africa and present day Saudi Arabia), converting rich grasslands into absolute desert, generating huge shifts in human population. Out of this chaos came our monotheistic God concept, that had to be projected onto the heavens above because things were so chaotic on the earth itself. And in due course, the violent rivalries invented by warring humans on earth also irrupted in heaven, concocting the story of the rebellious angels, who allegedly were kicked out of heaven and on earth became the progenitors of original sin.

One wonders how intelligent human beings could ever have become so gullible and so codependent! For some five thousand years, we have swallowed these outrageous myths, perpetuating belief systems that have wreaked havoc on people and planet alike. The philosopher Friedrich Nietzsche and several others have tried to kill off this preposterous God figure but not with much success. Our contemporary worldview, particularly as perpetuated by Western postcolonial force, is still too ensnared in a codependent consciousness. We are just not adult enough to let go of the infantile grip such religiosity holds on us and reclaim a more integrated spirituality within the living womb of creation itself. There we will encounter the Great Spirit, a far more liberating and empowering Incarnation of the true God.

It is only when we have undergone such a conversion that we can honor a quality of collaboration that is religiously empowering precisely because it grounds us more authentically in the web of life, more attuned to the living energy of creation where we have more unfiltered access to the true God.

Incarnation of Spirit

This chapter could be understood as laying the foundations for the revamped and revitalized understanding of Incarnation that constitutes the subject matter of this book. Thus far, three insights are emerging:

- God as Spirit is the oldest understanding of divine presence discerned by human beings and affirmed by several contemporary adult faith seekers.
- Humans made that discernment through a convivial relationship with the natural world, an intuition largely lost to contemporary humans.
- The primary agent of incarnational affirmation and empowerment is not Jesus but the living Spirit of God.

How much of our human alienation, and the ensuing deviant behavior, arises from this lost interconnectedness, our estrangement from the primordial womb, where we relished an intimacy, now subverted by our excessive rationalism, functionalism, and dysfunctional anthropocenticism?

How apt, therefore, for the liberation theologian Leonardo Boff to assert so forthrightly: "We will find the Spirit first in the cosmos, and only then in ourselves" (Boff 2015, vii). As we come home to where we truly belong as earthlings, we will not become more secular and materialistic, but rather more spiritually enlightened and grounded—in a word, more incarnated within the embodiment of the living earth itself.

In theological terms, therefore, the primary Incarnation we need to come to terms with is not the Jesus-based one but that which is grounded in that divine reality we name as Holy Spirit of God. That is where it all begins. Leonardo Boff (2015, 60) goes so far as to suggest that even God has his/her beginning in that same primordial truth: "God also belongs to the domain of the Spirit; it could not be otherwise." The hierarchical ladder of Father, Son, and Holy Spirit may not be as theologically sturdy as we have traditionally assumed. Thanks to the increasing and advancing multidisciplinary wisdom of our time, we are retrieving a deeper ancient wisdom that requires us to redefine everything, even our very understanding of God.

By prioritizing the Spirit, as the energizing source of everything in creation, we begin to face the enormous challenge of addressing other priorities. Most daunting of all is our own inflated anthropocentrism, which the renowned microbiologist, Lynn Margulis (1998, 149), mercilessly denounces in these oft-quoted words: "Our tenacious illusion of special dispensation belies our true status as upright, mammalian weeds." In a later publication, she added: "Gaia (the living earth) is not the nurturing mother or fertility doll of the human race. Rather, human beings, in spite of our raging anthropocentrism, are relegated to a tiny and unessential part of the gaian system" (Margulis 2008, 182).

That which constitutes our true nature as human creatures is not based on some privileged, exalted status as we have long believed, but rather on our ability to affiliate in a more integrated way with the earth we inhabit and the universe to which we belong. We are an interdependent species whose growth, development, and evolution are integrally connected with the surrounding web of life. Even those characteristics that we long assumed were ours by virtue of some Darwinian advantage— our superior intelligence, our soul-filled spiritual nature—we now realize were bestowed upon us by the surrounding creation. To quote Leonardo Boff (2015, 134) once more, "We have spirit and consciousness because they were already here in the universe."

In subsequent chapters, we will return to the anthropological intricacies of redefining our human essence and our integral place in God's creation. This all has several implications for how we redefine the meaning of Incarnation. While the reader may wish to move rapidly to these pressing human issues, we need to abide with the larger context. Having briefly reviewed our cosmic context and the energizing influence of the Great Spirit, we now need to give a more focused attention to our earthy dimension. *It is in and through the living earth that we honor and negotiate our allegiance to the Great Spirit.*

It is in and through our earthly organicity that we come to know and understand God's Incarnation in our midst, primarily through the Great Spirit, and subsequently through a range of other breakthroughs, of which the life and ministry of the historical Jesus holds a distinctive uniqueness for Christian peoples. How we appropriate and internalize the divine empowerment of this divine graciousness is also heavily dependent on how we relate with our earthiness. Our discernment moves on as we seek to appropriate a more informed attention to the living earth itself.

Chapter 4

The Spirit Embodies the Earth

Gaia's vision of Earth as a harmonious whole, engineered by and for the organisms that live on it, is a deeply evocative notion.

—James E. Kirchner

Vast in its analytic and inventive power, modern humanity is crippled by a fear of its own animality, and of the animate earth that sustains us. . . . We could never have survived as a species without our propensity for animistic engagement with every aspect of our earthly habitat.

—David Abram

Thus far, our reflections suggest that the primary Incarnation (embodiment) of God in creation is that of the Holy Spirit, more aptly described as the Great Spirit, long known to indigenous and First Nations peoples. And the primary embodiment of the Great Spirit is not some transcendent, ethereal phenomenon above and beyond the material creation. To the contrary, it is the living earth itself as a vibrating dynamic organism, energized by the creative energy of the Great Spirit. In other words, the revealed truth and presence of the divine reaches us through the living earth itself.

Our earthiness is the umbilical cord linking us to the source of our holiness (read: wholeness), through the earth, not in spite of it, and certainly not beyond it.

Despite the fact that mainline Christianity has long condemned and marginalized our earthiness, we are gradually becoming aware that the sacredness of the land was an integral faith experience of the Jewish people (cf. Habel 1995), a truth also to be discerned in several of the gospel parables. How the Spirit embodies the earth, and consequently incarnates in all earth creatures, I will explore by reflecting on the short but loaded parable of the man seeking bread late at night. This is how Luke narrates the story:

> Jesus said to them, "Which of you, if you go to a friend at midnight, and tell him, 'Friend, lend me three loaves of bread, for a friend of mine has come to me from a journey, and I have nothing to set before him,' and he from within will answer and say, 'Don't bother me. The door is now shut, and my children are with me in bed. I can't get up and give it to you'? I tell you, although he will not rise and give it to him because he is his friend, yet because of his persistence, he will get up and give him as many as he needs." (Lk 11:5–8)

Incarnational Belonging

Luke actually allegorizes this parable, using it as a rationale for persistent prayer. In its foundational meaning, it is a parable of Jewish hospitality, with the earth itself deeply insinuated in the ensuing message. In Palestine of Jesus's time, people often preferred to travel after dark in order to avoid the heat, and it was not uncommon for visitors to arrive unannounced. No matter what time of day or night one arrives, the Jewish norms of hospitality require that you attend to the person's need (Gn 18:1–8; Heb 13:2). There is no question of refusing. For a host to be unable to offer hospitality to a guest would be shameful; more importantly, it would bring shame not only on oneself, *but upon the entire village.* A guest is a guest of the community, not just of the individual, and to comply with the cultural (and religious) expectations, a guest must leave the village with a good feeling about the hospitality offered—not just by individuals but by the village-as-community.

The master of the house is known as the householder, often portrayed in popular Christianity as the boss, the breadwinner, the person in charge. In fact, in the ancient Jewish context, his primary responsibilities were not those we attribute to a patriarchal parental overseer. His responsibilities for care, provision, and protection extended beyond his immediate house (home) to the entire village.

The Greek word being used is that of *oikos*, from which is derived words such as *ecology, economy,* and *ecumenism.* The Lukan parable referred to above illustrates very clearly the cultural and spiritual significance of the *oikos.* It denotes the house in which home making takes place, but the hospitality required for empowering home making embraces the larger cultural unit, called the *village,* and that in turn links everybody with the larger ecological domain, typically described as the *bioregion.*

The sociological structure, therefore, is that of an interrelational web in which the person obtains identity by belonging to a household, which in turn belongs to the village (what today we would call the bioregion), which itself belongs to planet earth. The parable portrays an integration transcending humans and embracing even the earth itself. In this primordial, sacred understanding, the nation-state has no place; that is a later patriarchal development. We must also avoid any hint of hierarchical ordering. We are not dealing with a linear construct from the individual person right up through house and village to the planet and ultimately to God as the creator of all. We are witnessing a holarchical, egalitarian process, with an underlying dynamic of empowerment rather than promoting or fostering anything to do with hierarchical power.

Holarchy is a relatively new concept for our time. The term was originally coined by the philosopher, Arthur Koestler (1967), referring to a special type of organizational structure in which wholes and parts operate interdependently, following the scientific principle: the whole is greater than the sum of the parts, and yet the whole is contained in each part. In ancient Hebrew hospitality, the person has no meaning apart from the *oikos*, the home/family to which one belongs, and the individual home in turn is insinuated into the village, which in turn belongs to the wider geographical reality of planet earth (not yet carved into nation-states), and ultimately everything belongs to the universe.

Biologists often talk of nested hierarchies, sections within larger sections as in the Russian doll. It seems to me that what is being described is holarchies not hierarchies. Strictly speaking, there are no hierarchies in God's creation. Everything is programed to relate—through *holarchies*.

The World Council of Churches brought the term *household of the world*, or oikoumene, to the fore and in 1991 when its former general secretary, Konrad Raiser (1991, 87–88), suggests that the word *oikos* connotes "community, webs of relationships, belonging, and with life together." The ancient *oikos* is not just one social and economic forum among others, but rather the basic social and economic structure not only for the ancient world and the New Testament but presumably for every preindustrial sedentary culture as well.

Worthy of note too is the astute observation of historian, Kate Cooper, that in the time of Jesus three faith structures flourished, the temple, the synagogue, and the household, and in the case of the third, it was women rather than men who provide dynamic leadership (Cooper 2013, 16–17), an observation for which Osiek and MacDonald (2006, 144ff) provide detailed elaboration. In fact, several scholars maintain that in rural Galilee during the time of Jesus, the synagogue was not a church-like entity set apart but was typically based in a family household. And whereas it is men, typically cast in the patriarchal line that represent the temple and synagogue, it seems that it was women (and occasionally, couples like Prisca and Aquila [Rom 16:3; 1 Cor 16:19], Andronicus and Junia [Rom 16:7], Philogus and Julia [Rom 16:15]) who are the leading facilitators of the house-church in early Christian times.

This organic relational paradigm is the basis of how creation operates at every level, very different from the patriarchal carving of the earth into nation-states (most of which were created through the violence of warfare) and significantly at variance with the cold rationalism of mainstream science that views creation as a collection of discreet entities, a material object created for human benefit and usufruct. While this scientific understanding may have contributed to human progress, we are now realizing that it has happened at a high price for other organic species, including humans. In its ecological aspect, the *oikos* flourishes on a delicate balance of several chemical and organic processes. In its economic aspect, the household is a continual reminder to us of the essential giftedness of everything that endows life with meaning and purpose. In its ecumenical significance, the household is not meant to be an isolated entity vying competitively with every other reality, but rather a collaborative endeavor that celebrates commonalities rather than differences. And in its political significance, it is seriously undermined by subverting and fragmenting creation into nation-states.[1]

In the present chapter, I want to illuminate the incarnational significance of the living earth itself, as an integral dimension of divine embodiment. Here we touch on a meaning of Incarnation virtually unheard of among theologians, past or present.

---

[1] Many people—and most governments—assume that the nation-state is an indispensable institution, without which anarchy would prevail. The history of nationalism indicates all too clearly the problematic nature of such states and the enormous violence out of which several have been carved. And in a world becoming ever more globalized, the nation-state is proving to be a dysfunctional organization on several levels. For more, see Giddens (1985), Ohmae (1990), and White (2007).

Throughout this book, I frequently remind the reader of the close affiliation of Incarnation with *embodiment*, identifying bodies as the primary vehicles through which the creative energy of the divine flows and matures into a vast range of expressions. And such corporeal beings must not be reduced to human reality, nor is it appropriate anymore to view the human body as superior to all other embodied forms.

Let's therefore begin with this assertion on what the body denotes: "The body is a place where clouds, earthworms, guitars, clucking hens, and clear-cut hillside all converge, forging alliances, mergers, and metamorphoses . . . the body itself is a kind of place—not a solid object but a terrain through which things pass and in which they sometimes settle and sediment" (Abram 2010, 229–30). *The body is a process rather than a product,* an evolving and expanding horizon within which various elements seek out a more optimal climate for growth and flourishing.

As indicated in the last chapter, the Spirit is infused in every aspect of creation as its creative and sustaining energy. Without body, however, the Spirit goes nowhere; *it is in and through bodies that spirit becomes grounded and generic at every level of creation's evolution.* Here we are confronting a major shift of emphasis. Throughout modern human civilization, the human is regarded as a superior being, an inflated status fully supported by the formal religions, claiming that the human incarnates the divine on earth above and beyond any other organic creature. In fact, religionists of a more fundamental persuasion claim that it is only in and through the human that God becomes incarnate on earth.

In these allusions to the human, there is the further subtly of the soul within the body, or the emphasis on spirit over against material body. In this case, Incarnation pertains to soul or spirit (within the body) rather than to the body in its complex totality, including physical structure, social dimensionality, psychic faculties, and spiritual aspiration. Therefore, the human and religious preoccupation with the body, as a possible site of divine incarnation, has been something of a tortured history, full of ambiguity, confusion and negative projection.

Certainly, contemporary theologians, and people of other disciplines, seek to redress this ancient imbalance, first, by helping us to see why and how so many distortions arose and, second, by figuring out how to move beyond such limitations amid the awakening (adult) consciousness of the twenty-first century. My hope is that the present book will contribute to that process of rehabilitation. While the incarnational horizons that I depict will be dismissed by several academics (theologians included), I rejoice in the fact that several adult faith seekers will embrace this expanded understanding of Incarnation with joy and enthusiasm. They will embrace it, not so much because it is spiritually more cogent than former understandings, but because these insights resonate deeply with their spiritual search for meaning in the evolutionary context of the twenty-first century.

The Gaia Hypothesis

Let us continue to wrestle with this new incarnational threshold, namely, that it is *the material creation, earth stuff, that constitutes the ground of all holiness.* We grow into divine holiness not by escaping our earthiness but by engaging with it in a deeper more organic way. And that is only possible by a much deeper understanding and appreciation of the living earth above and beyond the crude materialism and scientific atomism with which we have been indoctrinated for far too long.

I wish to suggest that the outstanding scientific discovery of the twentieth century is not television, or computer technology, but rather *the complexity of the land itself as a living organism.* Only those who know much about planet earth can appreciate how little we actually do know. The earth is seen as a living entity—a Gaian worldview—and our obligations as humans are not just to ourselves but to all of life. Once we truly grasp the organic reality of our living planet and its physiology, our entire worldview and practice are bound to change profoundly—despite the fact that social, political, economic, and even religious forces will fiercely oppose such claims.

Gaia theory is a compelling new way of understanding life on our planet. The theory asserts that living organisms and their inorganic surroundings have evolved together as a single living system that greatly affects the chemistry and conditions of earth's surface. The Gaia theory posits that the organic and inorganic components of planet earth have evolved together as a single living, self-regulating system. It suggests that this living system has automatically controlled global temperature, atmospheric content, ocean salinity, and other factors, maintaining its own habitability. The theory was first popularized in the 1970s by British researcher James Lovelock (1979, 1988) and since then has been critically reviewed by a range of scientists.[2]

Somewhat similar to a human body's immune system, the earth body is endowed with an inner wisdom that maintains conditions suitable for the earth's own survival. Air (atmosphere),

---

[2] The Gaia theory was developed in the late 1960s by James Lovelock, a British scientist and inventor. What was originally a hypothesis (duly elevated to a theory) gained an early supporter in Lynn Margulis, a microbiologist at the University of Massachusetts. And since then, it has inspired many leading figures of the past twenty years, including Vaclav Havel, Joseph Campbell (mythology expert), Freeman Dyson (physicist), Al Gore, and Elisabet Sahtouris (systems theorist). In 2001, a thousand scientists at the European Geophysical Union meeting signed the Declaration of Amsterdam, starting with the statement "The Earth System behaves as a single, self-regulating system with physical, chemical, biological, and human components." In 2005 the Ecological Society of America invited Lovelock to join their fellowship, and in 2006 the Geological Society of London awarded Lovelock with the Wollaston Medal for his work on the Gaia theory. Despite some strong opposition, the theory continues to enjoy engaging research, mainly in multidisciplinary fields of earth-system science and biogeochemistry. Increasingly, it also features in studies on climate change.

water (hydrosphere), earth (geosphere or pedosphere), and life (biosphere) interact to form a single evolving dynamism capable of maintaining environmental conditions consistent with life. In this respect, the living system of earth may be compared to the immune system of any individual organism, regulating body temperature, blood salinity, etc. So, for instance, even though the luminosity of the sun—the earth's heat source—has increased by about 30 percent since life began almost four billion years ago, the living system has responded as a whole to maintain temperatures at levels suitable for life.

The incarnational significance of the earth body itself was further reinforced throughout the closing decades of the twentieth century by the experience of the astronauts; as they looked back at the earth from outer space, many experienced an unexpected awakening of planetary grandeur. Those iconic images of the blue white planet, and a string of mystical-type observations from astronauts of different cultures and religions, more than any thorough scientific analysis, generated a compelling conviction that our earth flourishes uniquely as a generic whole. The symbiotic cohesion of the earth body demands that we continue to look deeper for a meaning that, among all the elaborate theories, is also profoundly spiritual in its meaning and purpose.

This book aims at a redefinition of the Christian notion of Incarnation, one that will command credibility and meaning in the context of the multidisciplinary wisdom of the twenty-first century. Thus far, I am suggesting the Great Spirit, as understood in First Nations spirituality, should be considered the primary embodiment of God in our created universe. Additionally, our earth embodiment, informed by the insights of the Gaia theory, suggests a complex and intelligent organic process that has direction and purpose deeply inscribed in its daily workings. Long before humans came on the scene, the Incarnation of Holy Wisdom was at work in planet earth itself—leading inevitably (it seems to me) to the evolution of organic life.

What Is Life?

By prioritizing the earth as being alive, thus hinting at the idea that all life-forms are derived therefrom, raises philosophical and theological questions that undermine some of our clearest and strongest human convictions. Central to such convictions is the belief that life in its more advanced forms belongs to us humans and did not exist anywhere (except in God) before we evolved. In a word, life as conventionally understood, means human life, assumed to be superior to all other expressions of life on earth, and believed to be unparalleled in terms of what exists outside the earth.

Central to this superior way of being alive is the platonic notion of the soul. Humans alone have souls, and therefore are entitled to exercise an agency above and beyond all other life-forms on planet earth. Over the centuries this ensouled status came to be understood as humans having the right to regard all other life-forms as commodities existing for human use and for human advancement.

For the nonreligious scientist, the superiority of human life is identified as the endowment with self-reflexive consciousness (the ability to think about the fact that we can think), which is unique to human beings. Ours is a superior intelligence, they claim, beyond the capacities of all other life-forms, giving us the right and privilege to conquer and control to our own advantage, and to the benefit of the earth as we determine what would be beneficial for it.

In the midst of all this arrogance—deeply religious in its origins—is an unresolved controversy on what life actually means. A basic criterion for the empirical definition of a life-form is its birth out of natural selection, and its ability to replicate and pass on its genetic information to succeeding generations.[3]

---

[3] Consequently, Dawkins argues against the idea of Gaia as a living organism since the planet is not the offspring of any parents and is unable to reproduce. Lovelock, however, defines life as a self-preserving, self-similar

Evidence suggests that life on earth has existed for about 3.7 billion years. How it originated continues to be a hotly disputed topic, with some theorists still evoking the primordial soup theory, others invoking the fanciful idea of panspermia (life seeded from outer space), while the current perusal seems to favor an origin in the deep seas.

As indicated in a previous work (O'Murchu 2012), I favor a more cosmic evolutionary understanding, along the lines proposed by the British paleontologist Simon Conway Morris (2003, 39): "Rather surprisingly, it is now becoming increasingly clear that at least some of what we regard as the building blocks of life were probably synthesized long before the solar system itself formed." Insights from *living systems theory* are adopted today to explain the nature of life in a way that is more amenable to embracing insights from the triple structure of information, knowledge, and wisdom. Such a general theory, arising out of the *ecological* and *biological sciences*, attempts to map general principles for how living systems work. Whereas mechanistic science (and biology) is determined by forces and trajectories, evolutionary processes function in terms of change, growth, and development, requiring a new science of complexity. Instead of examining phenomena by attempting to break things down into component parts, a general living systems theory explores phenomena in terms of dynamic patterns of the relationships of organisms with their environment. The scientific principle of the whole being greater than the sum of the parts plays a central role.

In a word, life is a cosmic imperative (see Christian de Duve 1996, 2002). The earth's ability to self-organize, and maximize its own resources, to advance its growth and development, is understood to be a central feature not merely of the earth itself but of

---

system of feedback loops like Humberto Maturana's concept of *autopoiesis*; as a self-similar system, life could be a cell as well as an organ embedded into a larger organism, similar to an individual within a larger interdependent social context.

all living systems. Systems theorist, Harold J. Morowitz (2002) explains life as a property of an *ecological system* rather than a single organism or species. He argues that an ecosystemic definition of life is preferable to a strictly biochemical or physical one. Paul Davies (2006) pleads that we look at what life does, rather than expending time and energy trying to figure out what it is.

In incarnational terms, life is a process unfolding in the direction of greater and richer complexity. Although infiltrated through and through with the paradoxical elements of destruction, waste, and death, it nonetheless suggests an underlying dynamic creativity that humans name as *God*. If we could honor more fully the complex and chaotic unfolding of life, we would be much more cautious in attributing life to the highly personalized God who is more a projection of our own anthropocentric need rather than the cocreative life force at work in evolution. Re-visioning this life force in terms of the Great Spirit (as in Chapter 3) seems to be a far more fruitful line of enquiry than clinging to several of our anthropocentric notions of God.

Faith Incarnated in Earthly Wisdom

Life is a systemic unfolding process within the fertile and malleable embodied organicity of planet earth itself. Contrary to the materialistic significance employed by rational scientists and the technological philosophy of the age of Enlightenment, our regard for the earth as a compilation of raw resources waiting to be conquered and controlled led to a mechanistic view of the earth that is increasingly problematic even for the materialists themselves. The more we exploit and extract from the earth to satisfy human need, the less satisfied most humans are. By objectifying the earth as a thing to be exploited and bartered, we actually engender an alienation that damages and disempowers our potential creativity. By objectifying the material creation, we progressively turn ourselves into objectified robots fiercely competing for resources that forever become more difficult to accrue to the benefit of all.

Our relationship with the living earth has become highly dysfunctional. In our stance over against the earth body, not merely do we cause irreparable damage to the womb that sustains us, but we also undermine the very integrity through which fulfillment and happiness are possible. As incarnational beings, we are intimately and integrally related to the earth itself, and, in the long term, our very survival will require us to drastically change the dysfunctional dynamics we have adopted in recent centuries. The alternative more organic approach—and that which is also more conducive to incarnational flourishing—can be illustrated through a series of new awarenesses that have come about in recent times. I offer a few examples that provide valuable guidelines for how we might once more reclaim our incarnational integrity as earthlings.

The Contemplative Stance

In the Christian tradition, there is vast cohort of spiritual illuminaries who invite alternative ways of understanding the Incarnation from within the ecological ethos of our time. These include the great St. Francis of Assisi, Hildegarde of Bingen, and Meister Eckhart. In our own time, Douglas Christie (2013), theologian and specialist in ancient monastic practice, recaptures this organic inspiring vision, giving it fresh expression and context for our day. Paradoxically, Christie attempts his fresh synthesis from the lives and witness of the ancient Christian monks, whose seclusion and solitude did not separate them from God's creation, but actually immersed them more deeply in it.

Contemplation, popularly understood, tends to be associated with religious devotees, divorced from the frenetic realities of daily life and therefore assumed to be unfamiliar with real human challenges. This is a limited and rather false understanding. The renowned Cistercian monk Thomas Merton (1915–68) is rightly portrayed as an exemplary contemplative for our age. The more Merton experienced the seclusion of his monastic hermitage (in Kentucky), the more he became painfully aware of the major pressing issues, not merely in the United States itself, but throughout the entire planet.

Contemplation, in its true sense, is about the ability to see deeply, to view the world with a breadth and depth not normally delivered through popular media or conventional wisdom. To quote Douglas Christie (2013, 36, 334), "The aim of contemplative living in its widest application, is to address the fragmentation and alienation that haunts existence at the deepest possible level, and through sustained practice, come to realize a different, more integrated way of being in the world. . . . If the contemplative tradition has anything to offer us in this moment of acute loss and fragmentation, it is the conviction that this vision of the whole can be restored to our world." Life is viewed through the eyes of the heart, encapsulating feeling, emotion, and spiritual depth, and not merely through the rational view focused on cerebral judgment and functional purpose. Thus, the sacredness of all becomes more transparent, and with it the painful realization of how much life is undermined, damaged, and cut short by the limited vision of those who exploit earth's resources for human gain or economic expediency.

The Wisdom of Nature

There are those who contemplate the natural world and go on to translate their wisdom into poetry (Gerard Manley Hopkins, Wordsworth, Shelley, and many others), while others translate it into practical action, veering toward activism for ecojustice; these include John Muir, Florence Merriam, David Suzuki, Steve Irwin, Rachel Carson, Aldo Leopold, Jane Goodall, David Attenborough, Henry Thoreau, and Annie Dillard. While these are often the subject of intense social and political interest, and some have had extensive media coverage (e.g., David Attenborough, Jane Goodall), their alternative incarnational wisdom has not yet penetrated our economics, politics, education, or theology.

Those deeply imbued with such a love for, and practical immersion in, the natural world frequently are inspired by spiritual motivation. Dare I suggest that the Great Spirit lurks deep within their mystical awakening! I find this particularly compelling in the work and writing of the naturalist, David Abram. Born in 1957, Abram is an American philosopher, cultural ecologist, best known for his work bridging the philosophical tradition of phenomenology with environmental and ecological concerns. He is the author of *The Spell of the Sensuous: Perception and Language in a More-than-Human World* (1996) and *Becoming Animal: An Earthly Cosmology* (2010). His more recent book is largely based on a lengthy spell deeply immersed in nature and mystically entering into the inner creativity of other organisms, emerging with a radically redefined sense of what it means to be human:

> The story does not ask us to forsake the evidence of our eyes but invites us to look deeper, and to listen ever closer, feeling our way into participation with a palpable cosmos at least as alive and aware as we are. The jostling elemental powers that compose this animate cosmos are sometimes lucid and sometimes dazed—like us they must give themselves over to sleep, and the magic of dreams, if they wish to renew themselves. . . . That which transcends the sensuous world also secretly makes its home deep within this world. . . . Beneath the clamour of ideologies and the clashing of civilizations, a fresh perception is slowly shaping itself—a clarified encounter between the human animal and its elemental habitat. (Abram 2010, 298–99)

Abram's emotional and intuitive insights receive a strong philosophical and biological endorsement from Donovan O. Schaefer (2015) in his claim that it is *affect* rather than *language* that constitutes the foundational truth of religious experience, and may even be detected in the ritualized behavior of primates and other animals: "The linguistic fallacy misunderstands as merely a product of language, and misses the economies of affect —economies of pleasure, economies of rage and wonder, economies of sensation, of shame and dignity, of joy and sorrow, of community and hatred—that are the animal substance of religion and other forms of power" (Schaefer, 2015, 9–10). Contrary to the moralistic denunciation of earlier times, our animal nature does not distract us from the things of God, but rather it has the potential to ground us more deeply in an experiential awareness of how sacred the earth itself is, and how this contributes to our own sacredness as earthlings.

Biomimicry

If we can remain long enough—in an enduring contemplative gaze—with the complex life process itself, I don't think we can escape the organic empowering mystery staring us in the face at every one of life's turns. It takes a naturalist with the perception and immersion of David Abram to captivate the inner essence, the womb of our becoming, and the nurturing breast that provides our daily food, but also the creative vitality that awakens our imaginations, intuitions, and sense of mystery. Thus, Abram writes, "In a thoroughly palpable sense, we are born of this planet, our attentive bodies co-evolved in rich and intimate rapport with the other bodily forms—animals, plants, mountains, rivers—that compose the shifting flesh of this breathing world. . . . Sensory perception is the silken web that binds our separate nervous systems into the encompassing ecosystem" (Abram 2010, 78, 134).

When we become more acquainted with the natural world, and more importantly when we begin to internalize its creative dynamics, we progressively begin to realize that nature's wisdom also provides the ideal prototypes for how we should engage the natural world. This natural wisdom is known as *biomimicry*, which describes how we can imitate the models, systems, and elements of nature for the purpose of solving complex human problems. Biomimicry examines the extraordinary innovations of the natural world and the human inventions they have inspired.[4]

Biomimicry is an approach to innovation that seeks sustainable solutions to human challenges by emulating nature's time-tested patterns and strategies. The core idea is that nature has already solved many of the problems we are grappling with. The goal is to create products, processes, and policies—new ways of living—that are well adapted to life on earth over the long haul, and to this end animals, plants, and microbes are the consummate engineers.

Oft cited examples of biomimicry at work include the following brief sample:

- The sleek front ends of Japanese bullet trains are based on the long, streamlined beak of the kingfisher, enabling faster speeds while also resolving unacceptable noise pollution.
- A Brazilian beetle may be key to developing computers that run on light; termite mounds in Africa carry the secret on how to keep office complexes cool without air conditioning.
- Sharkskin has been used to make floor surfaces in hospitals and other public places that will prevent bacteria from taking root.

---

[4] The term *biomimicry* appeared as early as 1982 and was popularized by scientist and author Janine Benyus in her 1997 book, *Biomimicry: Innovation Inspired by Nature*, where biomimicry is defined as a new science that studies nature's models and then imitates or takes inspiration from these designs and processes to solve human problems. Benyus suggests that we look at nature as a "Model, Measure, and Mentor" and emphasizes sustainability as an objective of biomimicry. For a simple illustrated introduction, see Dora Lee (2011); for a more elaborate updated overview, with several practical examples, see Dayna Baumeister (2014).

- The Bombardier beetle's powerful repellent spray, used to ward off hostile forces, employs a low carbon impact compared with most human created aerosol sprays.
- Having studied the collaborative endeavor of bee colonies, Regen Energy created a new electrical grid into a communication network, capable of maximizing efficiency so as to balance loads during pricey peak power periods when electricity is expensive or unreliable.
- Polar bear fur has inspired the design of thermal collectors and clothing; the self-sharpening teeth of many animals have been copied to make better cutting tools.

Examples abound, as illustrated in the growing literature on this exciting and empowering discovery of nature's deep wisdom (Baumeister 2014; Harman 2014). It is not a case of science making new discoveries about the marvels of nature thus far unknown to humans. We are witnessing a paradigm shift on an earth body imbued with a wisdom many degrees more complex and empowering than human wisdom, reminding humans that there are more creative and dynamic ways to engage with life, strategies that are also far less violent and destructive than the ones we currently employ.

In incarnational terms, when we recognize how to engage our world in a more contemplative fashion, we witness the inspirited (inspired) earth manifesting in creatively elegant ways the divine will for life, a foundational organicity insinuated into every embodied life-form. We grow into a deeper appropriation of our incarnational faith not by the evangelical fervor acclaiming Jesus as Lord, nor by notional assent to a set of Christian doctrines, and less so by fidelity to a formal church, but rather by relating anew with the incarnational presence of the Holy One in every impulse of creation, within us and around us. Poets and philosophers elaborate on the glory of God radiant in creation; at a deeper level, mystics of our time engage the incarnational, embodied wisdom of creation itself, and seek to integrate it into daily behavior as well as into socioeconomic–political action of a type more likely to beget justice and enduring liberation for all life-forms.

A Pope of the Earth: Laudato Si'

In May 2015, Pope Francis issued an encyclical, *Laudato Si'*, adding a Catholic voice to the current precarious state of our earth planet and appealing to the international Catholic community to adopt a more proactive stance toward sustainable ecological responsibility. Although never explicitly stated, the time and message of this document is that we need to reconsider our place as earthlings, and adopt a very different approach in our management and treatment of the living earth. From a Catholic viewpoint, this marks a significant paradigm shift, a reminder to us that growth in any authentic faith for the twenty-first century must include a radical reappraisal of our status and significance as earthlings.

On closer examination, and behind the lofty theological language, the papal encyclical embraces and endorses several of the incarnational values explored in the present chapter, including

- Our earthiness constitutes our primary identity as divinely created beings. It is in and through our earthiness that the divine works most effectively and creatively in us.
- Our earthiness defines the context of our belonging, asserting that the earth does not belong to us so that we can treat it and dispose of it as we wish. To the contrary, we belong to the earth, intimately interconnected and dependent upon it for our growth and development as divine human beings.
- Our earthiness provides the formative womb of our becoming, as articulated vividly by naturalist, David Abram (2010, 110), "The human body is not a closed

or static object, but an open, unfinished entity utterly entwined with the soils, waters, and winds that move through it—a wild creature whose life is contingent upon the multiple other lives that surround it, and the shifting flows that surge through it."

- Our earthiness illuminates our sacredness. As we become more intimate with the organic earth itself, we feel and perceive the divine intimacy within all beings. Inescapably, we are challenged to encounter and befriend the Holy One, not in a heaven hereafter, but in the evolutionary revelatory power of the sacredness in which we are immersed each day.

- Our earthiness grounds us in the recycling web in which nothing is ever wasted, and all returns to its organic source to be recycled afresh. In this way we remain vulnerable and trusting of the paradoxical process of decline, decay, and death, preconditions for the new life forever poised to break through.

Laudato Si' (14) describes our world as a "sacrament of communion, as a way of sharing with God and our neighbors on a global scale. It is our humble conviction that the divine and the human meet in the slightest detail in the seamless garment of God's creation, in the last speck of dust of our planet." The encyclical goes on to call all Christians to change their ways, not merely along traditional moral and personal lines, but out of an ethical focus in terms of the living earth itself:

> It must be said that some committed and prayerful Christians, with the excuse of realism and pragmatism, tend to ridicule expressions of concern for the environment. Others are passive; they choose not to change their habits and thus become inconsistent. So what they all need is an "ecological conversion," whereby the effects of their encounter with Jesus Christ become evident in their rela-

tionship with the world around them. Living our vocation to be protectors of God's handiwork is essential to a life of virtue; it is not an optional or a secondary aspect of our Christian experience. (*Laudato Si'* 217)

Our incarnational faith for the twenty-first century embraces not merely a new focus on Jesus and the gospels, and not merely a rediscovery of faith in the church or in the human community. As *Laudato Si'* (202) reminds us, we are into a radical new appraisal of faith where the earth itself and its interdependent life-forms require us to embrace afresh not angelic-type dreams for utopia in another world, but a profound rediscovery of our vocation as sacred earthlings in the very earth we inhabit.

Chapter 5

The Spirit Incarnating the Human

The trouble with some of us is that we have been inoculated with small doses of Christianity which keep us from catching the real thing.

—Leslie Weatherhead

There is little or no evidence from the period prior to Christianity's beginnings that the ancient Near East seriously entertained the idea of a God or son of God descending from heaven to become a human being in order to bring men salvation, except perhaps at the level of popular pagan superstition.

—James G. Dunn

At one level, the logic of this book is quite straightforward. I begin with the cosmic creation (whether understood as universe or multiverse) where God begins in time; at this level the Incarnation of God in our midst may be understood in terms of the Great Spirit (as explained in Chapter 3). I then proceed to the earth itself, which first evolved about 3.8 billion years ago; as *earthlings*, we humans, experience the divine revelation primarily in and through God's embodiment in that creation (as explored in Chapter 4). I now proceed to the human race itself and what divine embodiment might mean in this context.

For the conventional Christian, the dilemma is already resolved. God's Incarnation in the human took place just over two thousand years ago in and through the historical person of Jesus of Nazareth; it has been achieved, once and forever. For the first time in history, God appeared on earth in human form; and for one clear purpose, namely, to rescue humanity from its enslavement to sin, caused by a primordial act of disobedience by rebellious angels in the heavenly realm. Prior to that rebellion, we postulate that humans lived like angels in complete harmony with God. According to this view, our original status belongs to an idyllic utopian condition, the harmonious nature of which was disrupted by the angelic rebellion in the heavenly realm. These disobedient angels were expelled from heaven and landed on earth, started propagating (via sexual intercourse), and thus sin is passed on sexually and biologically to all humanity.

It amazes me how many adults still collude with this myth or worse still accept it unquestioningly. It belongs to a consciousness that has little or no understanding of evolution, its meaning, and significance. It is further reinforced by a neo-Darwinian ideology, which claims that progress happens by adapting anew the successful patterns of past behaviors (a variant of the survival of the fittest). Accordingly, there is never any true novelty, only successful adaptations of what has proved most useful in the past.

Theologian John F. Haught, himself well versed in the vision of Charles Darwin, provides one of the finest critiques of this narrow, regressive view of evolution. Arguing for a more evolutionary perspective, Haught claims that it is not merely the drive from the past that directs the evolutionary process, but also the lure from up ahead. Everything in creation is lured forward toward greater growth and complexity (Haught, 2010, 2015).

Above all, our sense of God and the effectiveness of the Holy Spirit may now be reframed as we discern afresh the workings of

God in and through creation. God is not so much the governor as the goal of an ongoing cosmic process:

> Put otherwise, God creates and governs the world not so much by dictatorial management from above, or by pushing it from behind, as by drawing it towards a future of new being—and new meaning—up ahead. . . . The universe can become intelligible to us, only if we turn around after our long analytical journey into the past and look forward, toward the horizon of what is yet to come. What gives coherence, unity, and intelligibility to our still unfinished universe is not the atomized and diffused cosmic past—incoherence in other words—but the world's being drawn toward the horizon of a constantly receding and still indeterminate unity up ahead. It is in the direction of the future, therefore, that we need to look for what is ultimately real. (Haught 2015, 21, 27)[1]

Our Arrested Anthropology

Theology tends to adopt a similar focus: truth is rooted in the past, in that which has proved the test of time, located primordially in the idyllic state of the Garden of Eden, to which one day we hope to return. And the Christian Jesus is the only one who can make that possible for all of us. It was Jesus who initiated the universal process of salvation through which the primordial curse of original sin was undone, once and forever. Henceforth, it is a matter of following Jesus or choosing to remain in a state of damnation.

That resolution, however, raises a number of difficult questions, not least that of the several thousands of years during

---

[1] And Haught does not in any way deny the great paradox of creation and destruction that is central to all life flourishing, human and otherwise; for more, see O'Murchu (2002).

which our human species evolved on earth, prior to the time of Jesus. Till the twentieth century, it seems that nobody queried how long our species had been around. Even scientists acquiesced to a broad religious view that it was a matter of a few thousand years; and within that time span, the really important stretch was the time after Jesus existed. Although never stated explicitly, it felt as if everything that happened to humans before the time of Jesus was of little relevance for either God or humankind. And that limited view was further reinforced by Greek philosophy (particularly Aristotle) who essentially defined the authentic human by the ability to use the power of reason, and for Aristotle, that was quite a recent acquisition.

Philosophy and religion seek to separate humans from the enmeshment in the material world. By postulating the existence of a soul, as the life principle within the human body, humans can now separate from their slavish enmeshment in the material creation. This seems to have been Aristotle's notion of original sin: humans have been condemned to a kind of earthly imprisonment, from which Aristotle seeks to rescue them by adopting the power of reason and aspiring toward an ultimate freedom marked by the soul escaping from the material body.

Aristotle's understanding of the human seems to be based on an equally problematic view of planet earth itself, despite what many commentators consider to be an enlightened view of creation. Aristotle seems to have a very poor appreciation of the interdependence of all created life-forms and of earthlings who thrive through an organic relationship with the living earth itself. After Aristotle, both philosophy and religion are preoccupied with the notion of *soul*, and its potential fulfillment in a life hereafter, totally separated from the earth.[2] Whether intended or not, humans were indoctrinated into identifying the life beyond

---

[2] We need to note in passing that Aristotelian anthropology is all about males. Females are considered to be misbegotten males and probably endowed neither with a soul nor with the capacity for reason.

as the only real one. Therefore, what happened to humanity while on this earth was deemed to be of little or no importance.

Whether we attribute the flawed perception of the human to Aristotle's philosophy or to the later theory of original sin, perpetuated by St. Augustine (and others), our view of the human person up till the mid-twentieth century was largely devoid of incarnational value or significance. There then ensued a momentous shift, which many theologians have not yet come to terms with. In fact, many know little about the revolutionary new field, the study of human origins, known as paleontology (or what some name as paleo-anthropology), acquainting us with human origins going back an estimated *seven million* years.

In the present chapter, I seek to redefine the Christian notion of Incarnation, not within a mere two-thousand-year time span, but in terms of our long evolutionary story going back some *seven million years*. I ask the reader's forbearance while I try to clarify the evolutionary trajectory I am adopting. In this chapter, I have alluded to the lure of the future (as described by John Haught) pulling us forth with a tug from up ahead. According to this view, evolution is directed primarily by the lure from up ahead. Why then devote this chapter to unraveling the human story from the deep ancient past of some seven million years? The answer is because a deeper discernment of our past illuminates our search and empowers us in a more resourceful way to embrace the future with greater wisdom. In conventional Christian faith, we cherish the past, but it is proving to be a very limited, congested, and reductionistic past (namely the last few thousand years). It does not go deep enough. It fails to honor the grand time scale of God's creative Spirit, which has far stronger potential to open us to the Spirit-led future. In other words, a more penetrating view of the past actually liberates us for a more creative appropriation of the future. Let's then review the expanded human story and its potential for a radical redefinition of the notion of Incarnation.

Our Evolutionary Narrative

We pick up the story in 1959 when a husband-and-wife team, Mary and Louis Leakey, both paleoanthropologists, while searching for animal and primate fossils in the northwest of Tanzania (in Africa), came across the remnants of a human skull. Mary Leakey painstakingly extracted it from the layer of rock where it was found. The geologists accompanying the expedition advised that the layer of rock in question was two million years old and when challenged about that ancient date insisted that they were in no doubt about the veracity of their claim. Consequently, the human remains found there must have existed two million years ago.

The Leakeys themselves were baffled by the discovery. Even they were inadvertently influenced by the notion that humans belonged to quite a young species. Their doubts were warranted because, apart from a write-up in *National Geographic* in September 1960, they encountered among the international scientific community a great deal of skepticism. In fact, they did not succeed in having their findings published until 1964.

Until the 1940s, most anthropologists believed that humans had evolved in Asia, not in Africa. In 1891, an excavation team led by Eugène Dubois uncovered a tooth, a skullcap, and a thighbone at Trinil on the banks of the Solo River in Eastern Java. Dubois named the species *Anthropopithecus erectus,* arguing that the fossils represented the *missing link* between apes and humans; not until the 1920s were similar fossils discovered in Africa. In 1924, Raymond Dart's research team discovered a childlike skull, popularized and scientifically described in 1925 as *Australopithecus africanus.* Several contemporary scholars dismissed the finding as a fake, until eventually Robert Broome, a Scottish doctor who trained as a paleontologist, found the first adult *Australopithecus* at the Sterkfontein site in 1936. Broome went on to rename the new evidence as *Australopithecus robustus,* a transitional species between apes and humans.

While these remain significant historical precedents, it was the discovery made in 1959, by the Leakeys at the Olduvai Gorge—subsequently named *Homo habilis* (the handy person)—that launched the new scientific discipline, one that was to gather rapid momentum throughout the latter half of the twentieth century. The earliest member of the genus Homo is *Homo habilis,* which evolved around 2.8 million years ago.[3]

Homo habilis is the first species for which we have positive evidence for the use of stone tools. This breakthrough is known as the Oldowan lithic technology, named after the Olduvai Gorge in which the first specimens were found. (As indicated below the earliest evidence for stone tool technology now belongs to Kenya and is dated at 3.3 million years ago.) In highlighting this feature of *Homo habilis*, I am making my first allusion to the innate human capacity for *creativity,* the controversial claim of Kenneth Oakley's *Man the Tool-maker* (first published in 1949) and confirmed on much more rigorous scientific basis by Renfrew et al. (2009) and by Dietrich Stout (2016). It is that creative giftedness, and not some primordial flaw, that characterizes our human evolutionary story, with a creative dimension that dates back to at least three million years ago.

Homo habilis, therefore, should not be understood as the first to manifest human utilitarian skills, making tools for some human function or task. There is a great deal more at stake here, unearthing the human will to cocreate, the creative urge, which creation itself has bestowed upon the human who, in turn, will push the creative potential to a more sophisticated and liberating level.

Next, we encounter *Homo erectus,* the oldest known early human to have possessed modern human-like body proportions with relatively elongated legs and shorter arms compared

---

[3] In 2013, a fragment of fossilized jawbone was discovered in the Ledi-Geraru research area in the Afar depression of Ethiopia. The fossil seems to be intermediate between *Australopithecus* and *Homo habilis*; It has been dated to around 2.8 million years ago, making it the earliest known evidence of the genus *Homo.*

to the size of the torso. These features are considered adaptations to a life lived on the ground, indicating the loss of earlier tree-climbing adaptations, having now acquired the ability to walk and possibly run long distances. The most complete fossil individual of this species is known as the Turkana Boy—a well-preserved skeleton (though minus almost all the hand and foot bones), discovered in 1984 by Kamoya Kimeu, a member of a team led by Richard Leakey, at Nariokotome near Lake Turkana in Kenya; the finding has been dated at around 1.6 million years old. According to the journal, *Science* (October 18, 2013), a new male skull discovered at the Dmanisi site in Georgia is very likely a variant of the African *erectus*.

Homo erectus is the primordial explorer.[4] While *habilis* probably remained close to base, doing whatever creative activities stone work allowed, *erectus* pushed out the boundaries of curiosity and ingenuity. *Erectus* began to sense the vastness and complexity of creation but also seems to have been endowed with an intuitive sense that this was raw material for human use and ingenuity.

Next comes the species named as *Homo ergaster*, based on the skull of a mature adult who lived about 1.75 million years ago in Koobi Fora, Kenya. The discovery was made in 1975 by fossil-hunter Bernard Ngeneo. Not only did *ergaster* resemble modern humans in body structure but was more advanced in organizational skills and sociality than any earlier species. It is conceivable that *ergaster* was the first hominin to harness fire; in fact, it is now assumed that *Homo erectus* did have control of fire, as did every other hominin sharing a common ancestry.

---

[4] Early fossil discoveries from Java (beginning in the 1890s) and China (*Peking Man*, beginning in the 1920s), and at Dmanisis, Georgia (in 2013) comprise the classic examples of this species. Generally considered to have been the first humans to have expanded beyond Africa, *Homo erectus* is considered a highly variable species, spread over three continents and possibly the longest lived early human species—about nine times as long as our own species, *Homo sapiens*, has been around!

Most contemporary scholars believe that *ergaster* is an off-shoot of *erectus*, with essentially the same characteristics and capabilities. I detect a deepening of evolutionary significance, with substantial implications for our expanded understanding of Incarnation. *Ergaster* bears witness to a deeper integration of three key capabilities, namely, creative potential, an urge for innovation, and a growing sensibility to the giftedness of the living earth itself. The sacred is at work but not yet at a conscious level!

Homo sapiens. A 195,000-year-old fossil from the Omo 1 site in Ethiopia shows the beginnings of the skull changes that we associate with modern people, including a rounded skull case and possibly a projecting chin. The more reliable evidence for *sapiens* tends to be dated between 120,000 and 150,000 years ago. *Sapiens* denotes wisdom, *the wise species.* Not to be confused with some unique brain development, the wisdom referred to here is the awareness and understanding that evolves as earthlings engage the living earth itself and learn to live with it in a convivial, befriending way, as illustrated in the collection of essays edited by Colin Renfrew et al. (2009). Despite the fact that life would have been raw and brutal at times, *sapiens* knew how to read the earth's deeper organicity, engaging creation with a growing sense of mutual collaboration.

For contemporary humans, *sapiens* is the common ancestor, creating a relational base that modern anthropology has yet to recognize. I am referring to the developments in mitochondrial DNA noted in the 1980s by geneticist Rebecca Cann and her research collaborators, and first documented in the journal *Nature* (January 1987). These researchers claim that there was an original common hypothetical mother, dubbed Mitochondrial Eve, indicating that all modern humans originated out of Africa during a time span of 99,000–148,000 years ago (the out-of-Africa hypothesis). Despite counterclaims of both a scientific and religious nature, the theory continues to evoke corroborative support (see Oppenheimer 2003). While allowing for a degree of diversity suggested by the multiregional hypothesis, Mitochondrial Eve as a common ancestor suggests that we all evolved from one stock, with Africa as our common ancestral home. Whereas today we emphasize what makes us different, for most of our time on this earth, it was the commonalities we shared that defined our status as earthlings. In a word, the evidence for mutuality and interrelationality may be quite old, long predating the cultural differences and religious distinctions we cherish today.

These four breakthroughs—*habilis, erectus, ergaster, sapiens*—mark an undeniable progression in innovation, creativity, and exploration, important signals of Holy Wisdom at work in our incarnational grounding. However, they are not the oldest evidence available for human evolution. In the 1980s, Ethiopia emerged as the new hot spot of palaeoanthropology, as *Lucy*, the most complete fossil member of the species *Australopithecus afarensis* was found by Donald Johanson in the Hadar, a remote Middle Awash region of northern Ethiopia. This area would be the location of many new hominin fossils, such as *Ardipithecus ramidus*. Many of these older discoveries belong to the 1990s under the pioneering endeavor of the Berkeley researcher Tim D. White.

Our oldest ancestor known today is the controversial proto-human identified as *Toumai* and discovered in Chad (North Africa), in 2000, by a French team led by Michel Brunet. For this ancient ancestor, we only have a skull, but such is the sophistication and rigor of contemporary analysis; scholars have been able to identify several features that belong to the human (Homo) rather than the proto-human (Australopithecus). While officially categorized as *Sahelanthropus tchadensis*, it exhibits tantalizing clues for its closer affinity to the human stock, and today it is deemed to be the oldest human ancestor thus far discovered. For further information on the story of human origins (palaeontology), see Meredith (2011), Walter (2013), and my own synthesis in O'Murchu (2008).

Earthlings at Work

Three features in particular identify the transition to what we could describe as genuine humanity: the ability to walk upright, a brain size with a cranial capacity ranging from about 950 to 1,800 cubic centimeters (modern humans average about 1,400 cubic centimeters), and the ability to engage creatively with stone technology. The Toumai skull shows unambiguous evidence for upright walking, which suggests a dating as early as *seven* million years ago. As of 2015, the oldest evidence for stone technology comes from Kenya (East Africa) and is dated at 3.3 million years ago. Brain size has varied considerably over the eons, from 600 cubic centimeters in *Homo habilis* up to 1,250 cubic centimeters in modern *Homo sapiens*.

Contemporary studies in anthropology and paleontology still fall foul of the human tendency to project onto our ancient ancestors those behaviors we dislike in ourselves, as our lives unfold today. In the popular press, words like primitive, barbaric, savage, undeveloped, and uncivilized are still frequently used. Closer examination of the substantial evidence arising from intense contemporary research point us in a very different direction (cf. Renfrew et al. 2009). The more we unravel our deep ancient story, the more we encounter an ancestor who was highly creative, innovative, adaptive, and at home in the earth. And as we embark upon the *sapiens* stage (perhaps also in the Neanderthals), we encounter ancestors using fire, evolving language, ritualizing the burial of the dead (cf. Renfrew and Boyd 2016), exploring art, and traveling the seas. Progressively we engage the fertility of the land and the symbolic capacity of the human mind, while cocreating a range of complex social behaviors.

In a previous book (O'Murchu 2008), I made the provocative suggestion that while we humans remain very close to the earth, we flourish in several significant ways. And the more we discern how our ancestors relate with the living earth itself, the less evidence we find for anything approaching the notion of original sin, nor do we find any compelling evidence for violence and warfare—till a mere few thousand years ago. To the contrary, we seem to get it right most of the time. This all bears out the perceptive insight of Matthew Fox (1983) that we humans are first and foremost the beneficiaries of an original blessing and not the victims of an original sin.

We are earthlings to the core of our being. That is how we were born out of the dream of God, and if we understood our evolutionary story in a more responsible and creative way, we would see that it is our intimate bond with the earth itself that constitutes our holiness, our sacredness in every sense. Moreover, there is growing paleontological and anthropological evidence to suggest that the closer we remain to the earth the more we grow and flourish to our own benefit and to the advantage of all that surrounds us. In a word, the closer we remain to the natural world, the greater likelihood that we get right—in every sense!

The major corrective confronting us here is our problematic history of dualistic splitting: earth v. heaven, body v. soul, matter v. spirit, etc. This unfortunate way of perceiving and thinking came into force in the wake of the Agricultural Revolution (more below), within the past 7,000–8,000 years, and became a cultural norm during classical Greek times. Such binary splitting is unknown to our species for well over 95 percent of our human evolutionary story.

From this perspective, therefore, *original sin* is not a foundational truth, but a deceptively dangerous and seductive heresy that morphed into dominant myths like that of *Man the Hunter*, which according to Hart and Sussman (2005) developed from a basic Judeo-Christian ideology of humans being inherently evil, aggressive, and natural killers. We then end up subverting our long affiliation with the living earth, as gatherers rather than hunters, horticulturalists rather than avid meat eaters.

As incarnational, earthly beings, we get it right as long as we remain closely affiliated with the living earth, and we seem to have achieved that to a remarkable degree until a few millennia ago.[5]

Then came the dualistic splitting and the commodification of the earth itself, with an ensuing set of tragic dislocations leaving humans uprooted, disempowered, and alienated. In the words of naturalist David Abram (2010, 309), "An addled and anesthetized numbness is spreading rapidly through our species." It is at this disruptive juncture that original sin enters the scene. And the key point I wish to emphasize is this: it was introduced by human beings (voracious patriarchs) and not by God; therefore, it is up to humans to sort out the mess that we ourselves have created. Invoking a substitute divine scapegoat to rescue us through the power of the Cross constitutes a massively irresponsible human cop-out and turns God (and Jesus) into a blasphemous human projection.

Getting It Right as Earthlings

We earthlings do not need to be saved from the earth we have loved and cherished over several millennia. The first challenge facing us is to reclaim our true organic relationship with the earth itself. While we cannot do that with the full scientific rigor required by modern academia, we can do it with a realistic degree of credibility, drawing on the ever new evidence arising from anthropological research, particularly as we access it with intuition and imagination.

---

[5] This is not a claim that we have always gotten it right and only gotten it wrong for the first time after the Agricultural Revolution of some ten thousand years ago. Being creatures of freedom, with an impulsive drive toward creativity, of course we get it wrong, probably on a frequent basis. However, our closeness to the earth provides a symbiotic corrective safeguard calling us back to more congruent behavior. What that might mean becomes much clearer when we study the life experiences of naturalists, contemporary or ancient. For the present work, I recommend David Abram's impressive autobiographical narrative, *Becoming Animal* (2010).

Accessing and appropriating this ancient wisdom can only be done to a limited degree by rational thought and contemporary scientific rigor. When rational analysis is taken as the primary mode of investigation, we are likely to come up with a view of our prehistoric ancestors as primitive brutes, immersed in savagery and ignorance. From this conviction come theories like those of *Man the Hunter* (cf. Lee et al. 1968). The long assumed *violent* behaviors much associated with hunting and meat eating are viewed today in a very different light, thanks to the more creative research of contemporary scholarship (cf. Mithen 1990; O'Connell 2002; Hart and Sussman 2005; Fry and Soderberg 2014); to the contrary, it looks like we spent much of our evolutionary story as a horticultural, vegetarian species.[6]

Many, if not most, of our behaviors were nonviolent. Immersed as we are today in a culture of fierce competition, violent rivalries, and the international stockpiling of armaments, it is indeed hard to believe that an alternative nonviolent culture is possible.

A great deal of current research, however, supports and affirms an alternative view—the type vividly illustrated by the Australian evolutionary thinker, John Stewart (2000, 233):

> For most of the last 100,000 years up until about 10,000 years ago, humans lived as foragers in small multi-family cooperative bands of a few tens of people. These bands were typically linked into cooperative tribal societies of a

---

[6] Apart from the counter challenge within the scientific community itself—to the man-the-hunter hypothesis—we also need to remember the feminist alternative, voiced in the wake of the 1968 conference on our hunting heritage as a human species. Feminist anthropologists began to produce a series of articles and books with the countertheme of *woman-the-gatherer* (Sally Slocum, Frances Dahlberg, Eleanor Leacock, Elizabeth Fisher). The feminist critics were certainly taking issue with the concept of man-the-hunter, and not necessarily with the book's content since the latter had gone a long way toward reestablishing the importance of women's work and women's roles in hunter-gatherer society. Several writings of the anthropologist, Adrienne Zihlman, provide further elaboration; see her useful resume in Zihlman (2012).

few hundred to a few thousand people. The bands within a tribe met regularly and shared common beliefs and cultural backgrounds. . . . Inculcated moral codes and social norms that were passed from generation to generation controlled the behavior of the people within bands and within each tribe to produce cooperative organization. And the codes also organized members of the group to punish any individuals who broke the codes.

Unlike the more complex hierarchical human societies that began to emerge about 10,000 years ago, powerful kings or rulers did not govern the earlier bands and tribes. External management played no role in the organization of cooperation. A distinctive feature of the codes and norms that organized these tribal societies is that they tended to produce egalitarian behavior.

Often dismissed as utopian romanticism, and denounced as an archaic version of communism, this incarnational organicity deserves a more discerning consideration. It is not the case that we got everything right, which we never did. It is the growing anthropological and cultural conviction that prior to the patriarchal era of the past ten thousand years, humans lived much closer to nature and adopted the natural world as their wisdom and guide in most if not all their human interactions. Long before the science of biomimicry came into its own (around the mid-twentieth century), our prehistoric ancestors practiced this earth-centered wisdom through an earthly harmony almost totally lost to modern humans.

Once again, let me repeat, I am not in any way advocating a return to some idyllic past. One of the primary purposes of this book is to illustrate afresh the foundational link between past–present–future, with the past serving as a rich resource for alternative possibilities that, when appropriated, then need to be translated into the evolutionary context of the present time. And my particular interest in that process relates to the reframing of the Christian notion of Incarnation above and beyond the inherited Christian context, and how that aspiration informs the faith development of adult seekers in our time.

Our ancient capacity for ritual making provides compelling evidence for a species endowed with wisdom and spiritual acuity long before our so-called age of civilization. We have archaeological evidence to show that we buried our dead, some seventy thousand years ago, using elaborate rituals, indicating belief in a divine life force and the assurance of an afterlife. Neither sociological nor religious research takes this discovery seriously. This spiritual and creative quality of engagement suggests a very different view of humanity and Incarnation, devoid of much of the demonization and demoralization so common in mainstream religion.

Nowhere is our ancient wisdom more impressive than in the rich reservoirs of Ice Age art and its related expressions in places as diverse as Europe, Australia, Indonesia, and southern Africa (cf. Lewis-Williams, 2002; Cook 2013). The cave at Lascaux (discovered in 1940) and that of *Chauvet-Pont-d'Arc* (discovered in 1994)—both in southern France—provide the finest example of Ice Age art.[7] Similar finds have been replicated elsewhere, notably in Australia, southern Africa, and most recently (2014), in Indonesia.

From the time of their first discovery, a number of theories have evolved to explain the meaning of Paleolithic art. The first was, *art for art's sake*, suggesting that our ancient ancestors were

---

[7] Access to both sites is severely restricted owing to the experience at Lascaux, whereby the admission of visitors on a large scale led to the growth of mold on the walls that damaged the art in places. A facsimile of Chauvet Cave, on the model of the so-called "Faux Lascaux," was opened to the general public on April 25, 2015. It is the largest cave replica ever built worldwide—ten times bigger than the Lascaux facsimile. The art is reproduced full-size in a condensed representation of the underground environment. Visitors' senses are stimulated by the same sensations of silence, darkness, temperature, humidity, and acoustics, carefully reproduced to captivate something of the foundational experience of the original participants.

endowed with a strong artistic flair, an idealization dismissed by most researchers but deserving of more discerning attention. Next came the idea propagated by Henri Brueil that the images support the practice of sympathetic magic ensuring that the hunters would have success in the hunt; however, many of the animals depicted on the caves were not those hunted by humans at the time. Then there is the structuralist approach (founded by Claude Levi-Strauss) viewing the animals as mythic totems, a theory that never gained much credibility among researchers.

A new breed of archaeologist, led by Andre Leroi-Gorham, relied on the positioning of the paintings and their placement in relation to one another, studying the frequency of their appearance. This led to the identification of recurring themes, one of which is the *shamanistic motif.* Is rock art related to shamanistic rites; could it be illustrative of shamanistic rituals? David Lewis-Williams and the French researcher Jean Clottes believe the artwork is the outcome of people in trance states, induced by psychotropics along with dancing, drumming, and fasting. This is currently the predominant theory, although the case has not been made in a definitive manner, and the mystery of the cave art still remains.

Few can deny that with the emergence of cave art, some forty thousand years ago, something happened in the evolution of consciousness. The capacity for symbolic expression reached a new creative threshold. To delve into this mystery requires an ability to explore the prehistory of the mind and to trace developmental stages that stretch much further back than we have heretofore considered. The Blombos caves in Lesotho (southern Africa) confirm that people wore decorated and symbolic jewelry possibly as far back as ninety thousand years ago. Artifacts of artistic flair have been found in many parts of the African subcontinent, predating the major European and Australian finds (cf. *Science Daily,* August 27, 2009), the oldest to date being the decorated shellfish of Pinnacle Point (South Africa)—dated at 164,000 years ago.

Here the Incarnation of the human takes on something of a quantum leap, and those who have had the good fortune to stand in front of Paleolithic cave paintings frequently sense awe and reverence. Of particular intrigue are the *therianthropes* with the composite structure of both human and animal. Several are in similar postures with one leg raised in what appears to be a dance posture. These have horned animal heads on human bodies with their sexual organs prominent, often ithyphallic. In the shaft at Lascaux, we see a human body with a bird head. There is also an ivory statue of a lion man. These mysterious envoys have been regarded as masked shamans or as divine animal masters, as totems, as personifications of the forces of nature, and as archetypes of the ancestors that reach back before humans were separated from the animals. We seem to be standing at a cosmic threshold that unites animals and humans in a deep archetypal symbiosis, reconnecting us with a time when we were as yet undifferentiated from the powers of nature.

Animals feature extensively in the paintings, indicating a fascination that clearly transcends issues related to fertility or the hunt. It has also been suggested that people of the time believed that animal spirits were there inside the walls, half ready to come out. Painting the missing outlines drew forth the animal spirit, giving more direct access to the spiritual power of the animals. This theory has obvious associations with the possibility of shamanism and the celebration of shamanic rituals (the viewed adopted by David Lewis-Williams 2002), and requires us to hold open a range of other spiritual and ritualistic possibilities that time may yet illuminate.

Often associated with the European Ice Age art, in the upper Paleolithic period, are the Venus statuettes. The first representation was discovered about 1864 by the Marquis de Vibraye in the Dordogne region of France. The famous Venus of Willendorf was excavated in 1908 in the Danube valley in Austria. Since then, hundreds of similar figurines have been discovered from the Pyrenees to the plains of Siberia. To the modern viewer, some of the images look quite grotesque, obese, and exaggerated. Many interpreters agree that the affirmation of female fertility is a central motif. More controversially, some link the figurines with the possible worship of a female divine embodiment known as the Great Goddess (more in Reid-Bowen 2007). The possible implications for a re-visioning of Incarnation are substantial.

Salvation from What?

The Christian notion of salvation—as an escape from this vale of tears to a place of fulfillment in the hereafter—becomes increasingly meaningless as we reconnect with our story as evolutionary earthlings. We belong intimately to the earth, and therein lies our salvation. Our spiritual journey is not one of escape but of homecoming. Our alienation and violent, destructive streak arises from our separation from the earth and the misguided ideology that pitches us over against the womb of our becoming.

The spiritual task of our age is one of *homecoming*—we need to come back home to where we truly belong, where our creative God first cocreated with us and through us, where in ancient times we have long recognized that empowering source of Holy Wisdom, as the Great Spirit who animates and sustains all. Brought into our contemporary context, this is how the naturalist, David Abram, expresses the challenge:

> Our greatest hope for the future rests not in the triumph of any single set of beliefs, but in the acknowledgement of a felt mystery that underlies all our doctrines. It rests in the remembering of that corporeal faith that flows underneath all mere beliefs: the human body's implicit faith in the steady sustenance of the air and the renewal of light every dawn, its faith in mountains and rivers and the enduring support of the ground, in the silent germination of seeds and the cyclical return of the salmon. There are no priests needed in such a faith, no intermediaries or experts necessary to effect our contact with the

sacred, since—carnally immersed as we are in the thick
of this breathing planet—we each have our own intimate
access to the big mystery. (Abram 2010, 278)

In the closing decades of the twentieth century, the process
of incarnational, earthly homecoming took on a fresh impetus
as growing numbers of humans and agencies began to identify
and address the precarious state of our home planet today and
the several forms of ecological breakdown that confront us. In
some cases, this led to a new awakening of our cosmic origins
and earthly grounding as in the new cosmology (cf. Swimme
and Tucker 2011; Delio 2015), and the recovery of the long suppressed wisdom of indigenous peoples around our world (cf.
O'Murchu 2012; Spiller and Wolfgramm 2015). Even among
conventional Christian missionaries, evangelization shifted from
saving souls through education and health care to the invocation
of the whole person within the new agenda of peace, justice, and
the integrity of creation (cf. Bevans 2009; Miller 2010).

Ironically, amid those enlarged horizons, that of the human
species itself, with its unique evolutionary story of seven million
years, still remains largely subverted and unknown. Such is the pernicious poison of so much indoctrination around original sin, its
cultural contamination, and religious contagion that it looks like it
might take humans quite some time to get back on their feet and
begin to reclaim the sacred earthiness that is endemic to all we are
and all we are meant to become. How that relates to our inherited
Christian faith and the ensuing reconstruction that will need to
take place is the topic for consideration in our next chapter.

Embodiment in Cyberspace

We conclude the present chapter with some tentative reflections
on our current technological culture and specifically the impact
of mass information on our daily lives. Increasingly, we inhabit a
virtual world, where the very notion of embodiment seems to be

an evolutionary liability and a barrier to the inbreaking of a new liberation. British scholar Andrew Byers (2013) critically reviews the ensuing challenges, suggesting that throughout the ages, our bodies have often been understood as prisons from which to escape rather than as sanctuaries in which to dwell.

First, we review the technological implications often analyzed under the rubric of the *posthuman*. In its narrow meaning, it is often equated with the notion of the cyborg to denote the redesigning of the human organism using advanced nanotechnology or radical enhancement using various combinations of technologies such as genetic engineering, psychopharmacology, neural interfaces, advanced information management tools, memory enhancing drugs, wearable or implanted computers. In his futuristic projection, Ray Kurzweil (2005) claims that by the year 2040, we will be able to go into a doctor's office and receive a brain implant that can modify—as we choose—various aspects of our behavior or human personality. I suspect the facility will already be available by 2025!

Many people are not even aware of this imminent development, and among those who are aware, several will suspend any serious consideration of what is at stake. For people of a fundamental religious persuasion, the reaction tends to be one of apocalyptic doom, a world ensnared by the forces of evil, a sure sign that God's judgment is near at hand! Ronald Cole-Turner (2016), professor of theology and ethics at Pittsburgh Theological Seminary, adopts a more discerning stance exploring the interface between modern technological developments and the promising future envisaged in the Christian notion of eschatology.

What I am describing above is more accurately labeled the *transhuman* rather than the posthuman. The latter embodies a much more complex, fluid set of meanings elucidated well by the evolutionary scholar Ilia Delio (2013, 155–76), and by the feminist author Rosi Braidotti (2014), and the American theologian Ronald Cole-Turner (2016). For Braidotti, the *posthuman* encapsulates all that signifies the transition from the more uniform humanism of the Age of Enlightenment to the postmodern preference for openness, unpredictability, fluidity, spontaneity, and experimentation. Obviously, this has ensued in several creative breakthroughs but also an enormous amount of chaos, violence, and social breakdown. In psychological terms, we can detect a reckless abandonment of past behaviors and social norms that were felt to be oppressive and left many people trapped in dangerous levels of repression. It is that repression that is now exploding in our faces, and as a species, we seem to lack the spiritual, social, and cultural resources to handle it in a creative and responsible way.

It is a new evolutionary moment for our species, one with substantial consequences for the expanded understanding of Incarnation being explored in the present work. If we had the luxury to revisit major evolutionary transitions in the past, we would, in all probability, discover that the new breakthroughs of the time were generally perceived to be reckless, often viewed as horrendous; it must have felt as if the prevailing world of the time was falling apart. With hindsight we can now see that those transitions and breakthroughs were necessary for evolutionary growth and development. We can also appreciate that they did involve substantial breakdown of the prevailing culture and social norms of that time.

This is how evolution operates. I am not suggesting that it is driven by some form of blind ruthless determinism, as some Darwinians suggest. Rather it seems to embody a wisdom that we humans are not capable of comprehending, leaving us basically with two choices: (1) adapt so that we can learn to flow with it and thus become its empowered beneficiaries or (2) resist its momentum (which is what formal religion tends to do) and become its resentful victims.

So, whether we name it posthuman or transhuman, technology is central to our future evolutionary development, and to use traditional religious language, I will wager, that *this is God's will (desire) for us at this time*. We cannot reverse the technological breakthroughs of any evolutionary epoch; in fact, we have never been able to do that. The critical discerning question is how do we flow with, and befriend, what is evolving within and around us? And what is the wisdom we need to engage meaningfully and proactively? Unfortunately our patriarchal educational systems, competitively and rationally driven, and our religious systems, preoccupied still with salvation in a world beyond, have ill prepared us for this critical time.

Whether the ensuing technology proves to be beneficial or deleterious for humanity (and for the earth itself) largely depends on what quality of wisdom we choose to use in dealing with this new emergency. Thus far, the prospects are not good. We look to our politicians and respective governments to make wise decisions that will benefit us all; in some cases the governments look to the religions for guiding values. One senses a great deal of anomie and a lack of empowering vitality. An alternative wisdom does prevail: coming from the ground up, which all formal institutions fiercely resist and demonize at every opportunity. It may well be the wisdom that will see us through!

And that brings me to the cyberspace dimension of our age. This is often where the alternative wisdom finds a home, where our creative voices can be heard and opportunities for dialogue abound, albeit, cacophonous and confusing for much of the time. And everybody is jumping on board. Church dignitaries, politicians, and leading economists, on the one hand, and rank-and-file members of society, on the other, use Facebook and Twitter!

The communications technology of the digital age affords us vast opportunities to engage an unprecedented range of dialogue partners. Our tweets, status updates, blog posts, and online chats, however, are rendered as bodiless voices in the immaterial realm of cyberspace. Many are welcoming this new communicative era, waving such banners as the democratization of media and the utopia of unlimited connectedness. For others, our rapid embrace of new media is a leap off a sociological cliff. These critics worry that our online interactions merely leave us *alone together* and wonder whether our texting, smartphone-wielding teens will ever learn to communicate face to face.

What does the embodiment of God (Incarnation) have to say to the disembodied communications of our digital age? How can the Incarnation of Christ inform Christian media in a culture wherein bodily presence is increasingly minimized and our interactions are often mediated by screens? In our time, many also wonder whether digital technology has birthed a new way of life beyond the scope of our sacred texts and extrinsic to the church's theological heritage.

The rapid transitions that characterize the realm of cyberspace, with technology's own potential doubling and tripling at an increasingly hectic pace, is particularly scary for those who feel left behind, those who do not know how to keep up. And those who do keep pace (or think they do) inhabit a world where the fine line between fact and fantasy is ever more difficult to decipher. We seem to be evolving through a liminal transformation in which the sturdy structures of the past are all giving way to a world of quantum potentiality, perhaps, another way of apprehending Telilhard's *noosphere*, as Ilia Delio (2013, 168–71) intimates. A new kind of embodiment is enveloping us all, and to date our ability to discern its meaning seems very limited.

This new incarnational *structure* is as vast as the universe itself, the mega dimensions of which become ever more familiar to us thanks to the wisdom of physics and cosmology, while quantum physics and the mysticism of our time plunge us into the miniature depths of a world we suspect to be real but difficult to engage in a coherently wise way. Correspondingly, we need in every contemporary field of wisdom a breadth and depth of vision, largely unknown in previous times. In particular our current educational systems—at every level—are pathetically inadequate and urgently need a massive overhaul if our generation is to be saved from all-consuming ignorance.

Chapter 6

Christianity's Empowering Relationality

We need to imagine alternative modes of subjectivity instead of emphasizing autonomy as the goal of maturity.

—Kathleen Lyons

The institutional church has never been able to wrap its mind around the notion of relationship as an authentic spiritual path. But the fact that such a path has never been officially acknowledged does not mean that information about it is unavailable.

—Cynthia Bourgeault

The kind of religion we lack today cannot be found in the religious traditions of the past which are linked to static categories; what is needed is a new type of religion that can use all the "free energy" of the earth to build humankind into greater unity.

—Ursula King

Our proto-human Incarnation, dating back to some seven million years, evolved into the greater complexity embodied in Homo—*habilis, erectus, ergaster, neanderthal, sapiens*—bringing us into our present-day status of *Homo sapiens* (sometimes described as the Cromagnon), morphing further into the socially complex creatures of our information, technological era in a cultural milieu becoming ever diverse, multicultural, and postmodern. Some theorists even declare that we have evolved into a *posthuman* status, as technology becomes more deeply integrated into our well-being and advancement.

To some of us—myself included—it all seems so obvious: we are evolving into deeper levels of complexity and complementarity, and will continue to do so. And a central tenet of this book is that such growth and development is God's will for us as a species, and there is a divine incarnational affirmation to every new developmental stage of our evolutionary journey. In making that declaration, I hear panic reactions arising from several *orthodox* sources: cultural, social, and religious. And with self-righteous impetuosity, I am denounced as being a crazy postmodernist who has lost the plot in terms of being a rational, civilized, and responsible human being.

It seems to me that the *plot* is actually a cultural and religious bottleneck that could suffocate humanity to death. We are dealing with an ideology—a kind of cultural and historical blind spot—that is extremely difficult to acknowledge or to rework in a more discerning and empowering way. In our recent evolutionary history, I detect three developments that created the bottleneck, the first going back about ten thousand years to a development naively and dangerously described as the Agricultural Revolution; the second going back about five thousand years when *civilization* came to be identified with writing and urbanization, giving that word civilization a perniciously manipulative meaning; and the third, and perhaps most lethal of all, the anthropology of classical Greek times, exalting and inflating the conquering rational male. Let's briefly review each development.

The Patriarchal Worldview

Put those three factors together and we have what feminists describe as the patriarchal worldview. The underlying virtues are domination and control. The leading philosophy is divide and conquer. The ensuing religion is a king-like imperial God who makes a covenant with significant males and like them pursues a course of redemptive violence. The earth is an object to be conquered and controlled to the benefit of voracious humans, and humans themselves have become dualistic deviants who have betrayed the egalitarian collaboration that nurtured and sustained us for much of our seven-million-year evolutionary story.

Yes, indeed, a kind of original sin has come into the world, and it was not God who introduced it. It was warring violent males who perversely rationalized the plot so that they could lay the blame on warring factions in heaven who landed on earth and began propagating. Now the plot thickens even further, and we are only a few short steps from the patriarchal God who must intervene and violently sort out the mess created by the violent humans themselves.

To appreciate the complexity of it all, we do need to go back to the Agricultural Revolution, despite the fact that we cannot furnish the rigorous scientific evidence required by modern academics. As indicated earlier, this entire book seeks out a mode of discernment (reading what the Spirit is up to) that embraces wisdom bigger and wider than that of academic scholarship. Of all the books I have read on the Agricultural Revolution, I find Steve Taylor, *The Fall,* to be particularly insightful. Taylor, psychologist at Leeds Beckett University in the United Kingdom, locates the Agricultural Revolution in North Africa and in present-day Saudi Arabia (what he calls Saharasia) rather than in Europe (the more traditional view). As the ice spread down from Europe, it gradually eroded the fertile crescent of Saharasia, evoking from the leading males of the day a panic reaction that Taylor (2005, 124) describes as the ego explosion:

> The Ego Explosion was the most momentous event in the history of the human race. The last 6,000 years of history can only be understood in terms of it. All the different kinds of social and psychic pathology—war, patriarchy, social stratification, materialism, the desire for status and power, sexual repression, environmental destruction, as well as inner discontent and disharmony which afflict us—all these traits can be traced back to the intensified sense of ego which came into existence in the deserts of Saharasia, 6,000 years ago.

Environmentalist Richard Manning makes the controversial claim that agriculture is spread through genocide. The hunter-gatherer culture was quickly suppressed by the belligerent sequestering of land to grow crops and the subsequent domestication of animals (Manning 2004, 45). And with the ensuing dislocation came a range of infectious diseases unknown in previous times: smallpox, influenza, measles, illnesses such as syphilis, leprosy, tuberculosis, and a range of developmental disabilities in children and adults alike. "I have come to think of agriculture," notes Manning (2004, 119, 202), "not as farming, but as a dangerous and consuming beast of a social system. . . . Agriculture dehumanized us by satisfying the most dangerous of human impulses—the drive to ensure the security of the future. In this way we were tamed."

With the taming came the disruption and displacement of the hunter-gatherers' affiliation with the land, the desensitizing of the sensuous interconnections that kept humans grounded in the earth but also spiritually aligned with the emerging wisdom of the Great Spirit. The kind of embodiment that evolved with agriculture marked an incarnational shift from an egalitarian conviviality with the living earth itself to an isolation and inflation of the human, over against the earth. In the words of Robert Wright (2000, 79), "After agriculture first spreads across a region, chiefdoms tend to follow."

This regressive move is captivated by Oxford scholar Graeme Barker in his resume of the Agricultural Revolution, forging an insightful link with subsequent religious developments, not merely in Christianity but in the other monotheistic faiths as well:

> The transition from foraging to farming was the most profound revolution in human history. . . . Its legacy today is the mechanized and industrialized systems of farming that sustain extraordinary densities of population and a global economy that together threaten the sustainability of our planet on a scale unmatched at any time in the past. . . . The cosmologies that developed in tandem with, and that underpinned, the development of agriculture among prehistoric foragers, were the forerunners of the agrarian-based Graeco-Roman, Judaeo-Christian, Muslim, and Eastern religions, all of which have asserted the primacy of humans over the natural world. (Barker, 2006, 414)

The movement toward farming husbandry, involving the division and commodification of land, led to a new patriarchal stratification with an accompanying desire for logical and rational sensibilities, creating the second major deviation I allude to above. *Civilization* is a word used to denote all that is noble, true, and just, but it carries a dark shadow, rarely recognized or addressed. With the development of writing in the ancient Sumerian culture of the Tigris–Euphrates valley, and the first cities arising in Northern Egypt, the ruling male classes imposed more controlling levels of social stratification, centralized authority, military power, and the accumulation of wealth to the benefit of those in control. More disturbing still is the insinuation that everything humans were up to before that time (approximately five thousand years ago) was uncivilized, barbaric, primitive, irrational (or prerational), best left to that inferior age when humans were too enmeshed in nature and had not yet evolved into the maturity of *civilization*.

Our Deviant Anthropology

Thus, we ridicule and undermine the richness and sacredness of our long evolutionary story, and to our incarnational detriment we suggest that God was up to nothing good either, until civilized patriarchy redefined who the true God is (more accurately, should be)—a civilized imperial dominant male. And only civilized rational males can hope to embody anything of the incarnational integrity that belongs to authentic faith.

This brings us to third deviation, the most subtle of all, and extensively adopted in the culture of the twenty-first century, namely, our definition of a human person. Our current anthropology seems to be almost irretrievably influenced by classical Greek philosophy, particularly by Plato and Aristotle. For both of them, it is what differentiates the human from all else, and especially from the animals, that is critically important. And the key differentiating factor is the soul, which for both Plato and Aristotle is the seat of reason. And essentially that is what makes the human person unique—the ability to think things out rationally in one's head.

This emphasis on rationality is not merely a human endowment. For Aristotle it is a divine quality: "The human being is the only erect animal because its nature and essence is divine; the function of the most divine is thinking and being intelligent" (*De partibus animalium* IV.10 686a 27–29). In both the *Nichomachean Ethics* and in *De Anima*, Part 3, Aristotle writes extensively about human flourishing and the happiness (eudaimonia) that ensues. Indeed he views the human as made in the image of God (*imago Dei*). This is very impressive at first sight, and heavily endorsed by philosophers over the past two millennia.

It is the subtleties that require closer and more discerning attention. For instance, for many of the Greek fathers (inspired by Aristotle), the *imago Dei* resides in the nonsexual soul, not in the fully embodied human, and much more so in the man than in the woman. And these deviations cannot be explained—as many commentators do—simply by situating Aristotle within the biology and culture of his time. For much of the two thousand years of Christendom, Aristotle tends to be interpreted literally and still enjoys exalted status in scholastic philosophy; this is where things have gone drastically wrong for our understanding of the Christian notion of Incarnation.

For Aristotle, the human person is endowed essentially with four characteristics:

- *Autonomous*: Ontologically, we each stand independently on our own.[1]
- *Separate*: We are separate from, and superior to, all other aspects of the material creation.
- *Ensouled*: The dimension that links us with God, which no other creature has.
- *Rational*: As ensouled beings, we work things out through the God-given power of reason.

In drawing up this metaphysical anthropology, Aristotle was concerned primarily with males. Females were dismissed as misbegotten males, an unfortunate demonization that St. Thomas Aquinas adopted some 1,200 years later, a misogyny that still haunts many

---

[1] *Autonomy* is probably the most frequently cited characteristic in the contemporary understanding of the human person. Those who promote a culture of human rights, frequently underestimating (or ignoring) responsibilities and duties, strongly emphasize human autonomy, above and beyond other life-forms. MacKenzie and Stoljar (2000) provide a comprehensive and well thought-through analysis of this phenomenon, highlighting that the only autonomy that will serve humanity well (along with other creatures) is a relational rather than an adversarial one.

of the major world religions. But what is most demeaning in Aristotle's rendition—for which he is rarely if ever challenged—is his allegiance to the autonomous, robust, individualistic, heroic male as the model for all responsible and holy humans. It provides a grossly distorted picture of what humans were like for much of their long evolutionary story, and also the incarnational humanity that the historical Jesus exemplifies in his life and ministry.

Programmed to Cooperate

As a species, we are endowed with an inherited capacity for cooperation. Many among us are not even aware of that fact, and the fierce competition so endemic to our contemporary lifestyles leaves us with a deeply debilitating sense of woundedness. For a start, let's address the inherited ignorance around our true God-given nature. The capacity for cooperation is incarnationally inscribed in our physiological makeup:

> The cells themselves are cooperative organizations. Without extensive cooperation between the molecular processes and organelles that make up cells, we would not exist. Each of our million billion cells is made up of thousands of incredibly small and intricate parts that cooperate together to produce the functions of the cell. . . . We are cooperators that are made of cooperators, that are made of cooperators. It is cooperation all the way down. . . . Wherever evolution has been able to fully exploit the benefits of cooperation, we always find the extraordinary level of specialization and interdependency that results from a high degree of division of labor. We find it within cells, within our bodies, within our social systems, and between nations. And there is every reason to believe it will also be a feature of organizations that are capable of future evolutionary success on even larger scales. (Stewart 2000, 42, 45)

Our long human story is also imbued with this relational orientation. The ethnological data from hunter-gatherer cultures has provided a rich resource from which to surmise how Paleolithic hunter-gatherers structured their reality, living in bands consisting of fifteen to thirty people. Among our human ancestors, the hunter-gatherer band is the oldest known human social structure. There are still hunter-gatherer bands, but precious few, and many of them are threatened with assimilation. However, hundreds of examples have been studied in the past century. Researchers have found that hunter-gatherers live a life of economic, political, and social egalitarianism. All food and property is shared. Anthropological research indicates that at the band level, all members have the same political status and all are equal, and, it seems, there were no headmen or chiefs.

Political hierarchy doesn't come into play until society moves from bands to tribes to chiefdoms. In nomadic bands there is a natural prohibition on accumulation of material goods based on what you can carry. There is a decentralized system for distribution of goods, especially of meat. The band has built-in social devices that mitigate against bullying or selfishness. In Christopher Boehm's *Hierarchy in the Forest: The Evolution of Egalitarian Behavior* (1999, 69), he writes: "This egalitarian approach appears to be universal for foragers who live in small bands that remain nomadic, suggesting considerable antiquity for political egalitarianism." In Paleolithic times, many of our most fundamental values, practices such as ownership and private property, did not exist. There were no chiefs, no bosses, no headmen, no police. There was no money. Kinship was matriarchal. Monotheism, with its sanctioning of the one supreme patriarchal authority had not yet evolved.

"Hunter-gatherers, almost everywhere are known for being fiercely egalitarian and going to great lengths to downplay competition and forestall ruptures in the social fabric, for reflexively shunning, humiliating, even ostracizing or executing those who behave in stingy, boastful, and antisocial ways," writes primatologist Sarah Blaffer Hrdy (2009, 20). In fact, Blaffer Hrdy (2009, 38) goes so far as to claim that our propensity for cooperation precedes our acquisition of language (usually dated at one hundred thousand years ago).

The human capacity for cooperation has been long ignored (and probably suppressed) as a valid field for exploration. In our time, Matt Ridley launches a new wave of investigation in his 1996 publication, *The Origins of Virtue*, to be followed in the opening years of the twenty-first century by a plethora of new works, many of them rigorously scientific. These include the work of Sarah Blaffer Hrdy (2009) discussed above; Jeremy Rifkin's acclaimed volume, *The Empathic Civilization* (2010), highlighting the coevolution of empathy and entropy in our time; Frans de Waal's, *The Age of Empathy* (2010), tracing our cooperative streak right back to some of our animal and primate ancestors; Christopher Boehm's *Moral Origins* (2012), arguing that an ancient form of radical egalitarianism underpins our moral conscience; and Samuel Bowles and Herbert Gintis (2013), providing a scholarly genetic-based analysis of how cooperation and altruistic concern evolved in our species.

And this too is what incarnational humanity denotes. Since the gospel writers themselves were victims of Aristotle's distorted anthropology, they fail to deliver the incarnational humanity that Jesus illuminates for all who follow the Christian way. We get a glimpse of that alternative incarnational humanity in the gospel scene described in Luke 7:19–20 (parallel of Matthew 11:2–3), in which John the Baptist from his prison cell sent two disciples to ask Jesus, "Are you the one who is to come, or should we expect someone else?"[2]

---

[2] Knowing John the Baptist to have been an ardently loyal follower of Jesus, and declaring his divine status at the baptismal scene, Christians have been understandably perplexed by John's apparent doubt and anxiety. Scholars have tried to resolve the dilemma by offering one or all of these explanations:

Did John like others at the time of Jesus expect the promised Messiah to be a political-type deliverer, and was John growing impatient because the breakthrough was not happening as fast as he had hoped? Jesus was spending time with the poor people, those who had been marginalized, those who were destitute. He was teaching them about God's love, proclaiming the imminent New Reign of God, while healing and restoring their broken lives. On the surface, he wasn't trying to claim political power. He wasn't confronting Herod. He certainly wasn't adopting or supporting a violent attack on the Romans.

And to John's disciples, Jesus gives this response: "Go and tell John what you have heard and seen. The blind are now able to see, and the lame can walk. People with leprosy are being healed, and the deaf can hear. The dead are raised to life, and the poor are hearing the good news. God will bless everyone who doesn't reject me because of what I do" (Matt 11:4-6, CEV version). These words are generally interpreted as the Messianic promise outlined in Isaiah 35 and 42, indicating that Jesus indeed

---

(1) Most of the early church leaders couldn't deal with the concept of a doubting John, so they argued that John is trying to reassure his disciples to hold on to their faith that Jesus was indeed the Messiah.

(2) Although the gospels assure us that John knew Jesus's identity at the river Jordan, some wonder if this was more of an idyllic/mystical experience, whereas in fact, John's faith in Jesus is only progressively growing and developing.

(3) Still, others argue that being in prison could have depressed John and that he just needed reassurance. But John was a pretty strong character (it seems), so capitulating to depression seems unlikely.

(4) Some argue that John's question was one of *impatience* with Jesus because he was not delivering the liberation many expected of him.

(4) Others claim that John was *puzzled* because he had different expectations of the Messiah, perhaps similar to those expressed by the two disciples on the road to Emmaus ("We expected him to be the one who would set Israel free.").

(5) Finally, some wonder if John was *disappointed* in Jesus because he wasn't doing what John expected him to do, namely, overthrow Herod.

is the expected Messiah, thus reassuring John and his disciples in the face of their fears and doubts. We are not told how John felt about this response.

Taken at its face value, the text evokes this quality of rational response. But can we be sure that rationality is the appropriate vein in which to read either the question from John, or, more particularly, the response from Jesus? Among other things, we are dealing with a question of *identity*. Effectively, the disciples are asking, "Who exactly are you?" Throughout the gospels, Jesus engages questions of identity with the rhetoric of parable rather than rational speech. Why not adopt the same strategy here?

A rational answer to the question would ensue in Jesus pointing the finger to himself and, in loyalty to Aristotelian expectation, describing himself as the Messiah or adopting a set of characteristics to illuminate his God-given mission. As Robert Funk (1996) suggested many years ago, the direction of the pointing finger may be highly suggestive and rich in symbolic meaning. Jesus points the finger *away* from himself and not toward himself. And what does he point it toward?

"The blind see, the deaf hear": is this not the New Reign of God taking shape? Is Jesus not pointing his finger directly at the Companionship of Empowerment, my proposed renaming of the Kingdom of God (see Chapter 2)? So, what is he actually saying to the disciples of John? "*Stop looking at me the individual savior, and look instead toward my relational matrix, the web of my mission, from which I the individual Jesus—and you too—receives the divine mandate.*" Is Jesus confronting the disciples of John with a whole new sense of what it means to be a person: relational, inclusive, and empowering? Is he not challenging the disciples to cease gaping at some divine isolated hero (influenced by Greek philosophy), and look instead at the empowering divine presence in their midst embodied in the communal web of creation itself? Is this not what scripture scholar Marcus Borg has in mind in his frequent allusions to "the community that is Jesus"?

Relationality and Empowerment

And once we begin to glimpse that Jesus does not support the Aristotelian anthropology, and indeed contests it to its very core, we now need to engage an alternative parabolic wisdom that takes us to whole new levels of incarnational becoming.

In addressing the disciples of John, Jesus points the finger away from himself. What is he pointing at, or pointing toward? Some years ago, the scripture scholar Robert Funk (1996, 305) asked precisely this question, and this was his response:

> Jesus pointed to something he called God's domain, something he did not create, something he did not control. I want to discover what Jesus saw, or heard, or sensed that was so enchanting, so mesmerizing, so challenging that it held Jesus in its spell. And I do not want to be misled by what the followers did: instead of looking to see what he saw, the devoted disciples tended to stare at the pointing finger. Jesus himself should not be, must not be, the object of faith. That would be to repeat the idolatry of the first believers.

God's domain! The gospels call it the *Kingdom of God*, a direct translation from the Greek *Basileia tou Theou*. To the best of our knowledge, Jesus spoke Aramaic, not Greek, and the likely Aramaic word *Malkuta* has very different significance from the Greek and English notion of Kingdom. Instead of the imperial connotation, the rulership from on high requiring submissive obedience down through the hierarchical layers, *Malkuta* denotes mutual empowerment, whereby power is shared and dispensed for the benefit of the receiver rather than the giver. There is a significant shift toward giving away one's power rather than clinging to it for one's own benefit.

In previous works (O'Murchu 2012, 2014b), I take the liberty of translating the phrase *Kingdom of God* with words that stand a better chance of honoring the primordial meaning, namely, *the Companionship of Empowerment*; initially, I borrow the phrase from scripture scholar John Dominic Crossan (1991, 421–22). If we take that renaming as the primary inspiration and challenge of our Christian faith, then the command to "Seek first the New Reign of God" (Matt 6:33) takes on a dramatically new meaning, requiring a comprehensive reexamination of what we mean by Incarnation (cf. Howard-Brook, 2010, 407–17).

So the disciples of John faced a double challenge: (1) they, like all who adopt the gospel way, must seek *first* the new companionship, and their inspiration must be that of relational personhood and not the individual heroic Aristotelian prototype; and (2) more precisely then, this is what Jesus is saying to the disciples of John: "Don't be staring at me, the individual Jesus, but contemplate the relational matrix that is unfolding in and around me (the new companionship taking shape and expression). And as you contemplate that phenomenon you will begin to see what defines and constitutes the kind of person I am—at all times the sum of my relationships!"

It seems to me that Jesus never adopted the Aristotelian understanding of the human person and pushed the Hebrew notion of the human, made in the image of God, to levels that neither Jewish nor Christian researchers have acknowledged. For Jesus, the only authentic model of the incarnate human is that of relational becoming, an understanding of that time that seems to have been very original. While Hebrew anthropology embodies none of the dualistic splitting introduced in later Hellenistic times, and views mankind within the sacredness of the earth itself, it seems to view the person as a single unified entity, subsistent in its own right. Jesus made a significant shift beyond that appropriation of individualized identity.

John Shelby Spong (2016, 134) claims that Paul's extensive use of the notion of *righteousness*, frequently used in the letter to the Romans, is Paul's equivalent to the gospel notion of the Kingdom of God, with the central focus on right relating, in the name of love, justice, liberation, and empowerment. I quote a length from Spong's elaborated description of the Kingdom:

> The kingdom of God comes when we are empowered to live fully, to love wastefully and to be all that we are capable of being. It means that the work of the kingdom of God is the work of enhancing human wholeness; . . . It means that the work of the kingdom of God is done when the eyes of the blind are opened to see reality undistorted by religious propaganda and the ears of the deaf are opened to listen to truth even when it threatens our religious security. It means that the limbs of the twisted, the crippled and the broken will be able to leap with joy as new humanity breaks in upon us without the distortions of our tribal past. It means that the voices of those once muted by fear can sing as they watch all the life-denying prejudices that separate human beings into destructive camps fade away and die. That will be the time when the kingdom of God becomes visible, and that will be when God's righteousness—for which, without always knowing it, human beings have both hungered and thirsted—will finally be revealed. (Spong 2016, 140)

It is the novel relational dimension that seems unique to Christianity, which unintentionally or otherwise seems to have morphed into what came to be known as the doctrine of the Trinity in the fourth century. Long before that doctrine came to be formulated, with its complex metaphysical components, the historical Jesus had pioneered a relational empowering mode of personhood, which our theology of the Incarnation has neglected for far too long. Worthy of note however, are the contributions of two Catholic theologians of the mid-twentieth century, John Courtney Murray (d. 1967), and the renowned Jesuit Karl

Rahner (d.1984), whose attempts at a more relational understanding of the human person have been compared and collated by Gregory Brett (2013).

Our Anthropocentric Reductionism

As indicated in Chapter 5 humans have inhabited the earth for an estimated seven million years, and for most of that time, we lived in a convivial relationship with the earth, of a depth and quality unknown to contemporary humans. For far too long we moderns have been projecting onto our ancient ancestors all the horrible things we don't like about ourselves, failing to realize that these *sinful* tendencies have not arisen because of some fantasized battle in the heavenly realm but because of our own betrayal of our foundational embeddedness in the womb of the earth itself. In seeking to transcend our earthiness, we have demonized the source and sustenance of our daily lives. By claiming to be ensouled creatures over against the womb of our origins, we have undermined (almost to the point of total destruction) the very foundations of our earthly and cosmic integrity, thus creating a self-deluded monstrosity hell bent on self-destruction.

The social theorist, Jeremy Rifkin (2009, 18), highlights the same distortion, while forthrightly challenging us to address the dilemma we have inherited:

> Is it possible that human beings are not inherently evil or intrinsically self-interested and materialistic, but are of a very different nature—an empathic one—and that all of the other drives that we have considered to be primary—aggression, violence, selfish behaviour, acquisitiveness—are in fact secondary drives that flow from the repression or denial of our most basic instinct.

Religion has got the whole thing drastically wrong. We tend to forget (if we were ever aware of the fact) that the formal religions we know today all emerged under the shadow side of the Agri-cultural Revolution, that distorted development in which we turned the land itself into a commodity to be sold and bartered, and set up ourselves as functional manipulators, in place of being the organic collaborators we had been for thousands of years previously. And so deluded had we become that we began to postulate that God himself was also on our side, endorsing from above the sky our patriarchal strategy of divide and conquer.

I suggest we call that patriarchal deviation *original sin*, as British scholar Steve Taylor (2005) intimates. In this case, original sin is not a fundamental flaw that was there from the begin-ning, but rather a historical, cultural deviation that we ourselves invented, a by-product of patriarchal religious idolatry. It has nothing to do with God, other than with the false patriarchal God who embodies our own inflated projections.

And in our ancient organic conviviality with the earth, pain and suffering do not seem to have caused the alienation we experience today. We were not bent on ridding the world of *evil*; instead we befriended it as a necessary paradox to the mystery within which we lived and flourished. Obviously, our ancient ancestors could not describe this experience as we do today (thanks to our different way of seeing and understanding our world), but they seem to have been endowed with an intui-tive sense of meaning that our excessively rationalized world has largely lost. And that is at the root of the anomie, estrangement, and alienation contemporary people experience on a global scale.

Human Alienation

We have long assumed that our alienation is the result of original sin, an estrangement from God. And we are forever waiting to have it rectified, despite the theoretical claim that such a resolu-tion has happened through the death and Resurrection of Jesus. There isn't much evidence for that outcome around our contem-porary troubled and violent world.

Making God the subject of our alienation is one of the biggest blunders we humans have ever made. To one degree or another, all the religions claim that the God we believe in is a God of unconditional love. This, I wish to suggest, is an ancient primordial conviction, a kind of mystical intuition that long preceded the post-Agricultural rise of what Steve Taylor (2005) calls "the inflated ego." For many, the term *unconditional love* is an illusive, esoteric term, and certainly one we cannot make rational sense of, other than recalling those moments of deep intimacy, trust, or friendship when we knew we were totally accepted as we were, and there was no need to explain or defend the experiential moment. (I am assuming that most if not all the readers of this book have had such experiences, if only fleetingly.)

Whatever else unconditional love means, it denotes a quality of acceptance that is beyond the kind of judgment measured by human approval or rejection. It is a glimpse, however incomplete, of the sheer rightness of everything we are and everything that surrounds us in the relational web of life. It is an experience of existential grounding that transcends all words and explanations, reassuring us that come what may, the mystery within which we are held is fundamentally benign.

In this *sacred* moment, there are no traces of alienation, estrangement, or a feeling of being exiled from *God* the ultimate source of meaning and purpose. All is okay; in fact, better than okay.

The reader may have already guessed the goal of my argument. Assuming for a moment that our ancient ancestors got it right (see Chapter 5), especially in their experience of God's unconditional love, then it seems to me that God (by whatever name we use) is NOT the problem. One cannot be alienated from one that shows unconditional love; it is simply impossible. God is not the source or the cause of our alienation, and neither is God the resolution for it. In a word, it is not God's problem. It is OUR problem. Let's try to become *adult* enough to face that challenge!

The fundamental alienation we experience within and around us arises primarily from our faulty, dysfunctional relationship with *the creation of which we are a part*. As earthlings, we have lost the plot on how to relate rightly with the living earth, out of which we are born and upon which we depend every instant for meaning, survival, and dare I say, love!

Our compulsive drivenness to conquer and control what is within and around us is the source of our anguish, pain, and estrangement. This addiction to inflated power is a direct consequence of the dysfunctional anthropology critiqued earlier in this chapter. And we created this problem for ourselves when we betrayed our ancient convivial relationship with the living earth itself (the shadow-side of the Agricultural Revolution). God is only part of the problem, to the degree that we insist on playing God in our insatiable drive to divide and conquer.

The God who scares and frightens us, the God we set up as judge and king, the God who has tortured so many people with guilt and shame, is a projection of our own addiction for power and domination. And what we want to conquer is not sin and immorality, nor other people who disagree with us, but rather the living web of life itself. That is the core of our alienation and estrangement.

Millions have spent endless hours besieging a crucified Savior for comfort, consolation, and new-found freedom. The devotion is a misplaced form of codependency, a kind of cultural regression by a species that has lost its way, when it abandoned or betrayed the more convivial way of relating outlined above. And in our deluded alienation, we seek external redeemers to rescue us from a problem that we ourselves have invented. Neither Christianity, nor any other religion, has a utopian escape to a world hereafter; that is an interpretation long perpetuated by alienated people clutching to an alien understanding of God— itself arising from a human species alienated from the organic web of life itself.

We return, therefore, to the observation of scripture scholar John Dominic Crossan (2010) that our waiting for some divine rescue is no longer responsible in terms of an incarnational faith for contemporary adult faith seekers. We are waiting for God's intervention, *but God in Christ is waiting for our collaboration.* The intervention has already happened in the affirmation, confirmation, and celebration outlined in Chapter 5. Jesus has left us the legacy of empowering discipleship, and it is now up to us, the body of Christ on earth today, to get on with it. What we are called to redeem is not the aftermath of a Calvary of long ago, but the several crucifixions that reap havoc on our existence today! And our response must not be based on appealing to the sacrificial victim on the Cross, but rather by invoking the empowering vision of the gospels to activate the justice and liberation proclaimed unambiguously in the vision of God's New Reign (the new companionship) and lived so radically by the historical Jesus.

A New Evolutionary Threshold

We now need to integrate two dimensions of our inherited evolutionary wisdom: first our long evolutionary story that Christian theology (to date) has largely if not totally ignored and, second, the suppressed or neglected anthropology that characterizes the foundational stratum of our Christian faith.

Let's revisit our evolutionary story. Every catechism ever written seeks to reassure us that God is fully at work in creation at every stage of evolution's journey. Presumably then, our God was fully there when we first emerged as a distinctively new life-form about seven million years ago in the savannahs of East Africa. It is against this background that we need to hear afresh the recurring phrase in the book of Genesis: *And God saw that it was good!* Moreover we also need to acknowledge God's accompanying love and guidance throughout the entire trajectory of that long story. Of course, we did not always get it right; to the contrary, we got it drastically wrong at times, but on the big scale, we continued to grow into greater complexity (evolution's primary goal), and I want to run with the notion that despite our occasional faults and failures, we did get it right most of the time; and, in all probability, we did fulfill the divine plan for our becoming.

I appreciate that this is a huge claim that few modern commentators (in any field of science or learning) would wish to make, because we are so indoctrinated into the idea that all our previous evolutionary developments were based on a primitive, precivilized instinct that modern humans have transcended. As a species, we have created huge barriers to being able to see any positive or constructive truth in our evolving story. This is a grossly irresponsible prejudice we need to overcome and discard.

In my exploration of the spiritual and theological significance of our long evolutionary story (O'Murchu 2008), I frequently assert that we, for most of the time, got it right! Not surprisingly, most reviewers consider that to be an outrageous claim. Why do I make it? Because my perception is that up to the time of the Agricultural Revolution (some ten thousand years ago)—in other words for about 95 percent of our time on earth—we remained very close to surrounding creation and lived out a convivial relationship with the living earth itself. And when we humans do that, we tend to get right.

How come? Because that, it seems, is how we have been cocreated—in both divine and human terms! We are EARTH-LINGS! At every level of our being, we are programmed to live interdependently with the living earth itself. Our entire growth and development are dependent upon this foundational relationship. This is how we are molded and shaped by the divine creative source. We are God's work of art, carved out of the living earth itself, and not merely on the basis of some immaterial ensoulment. And we honor that foundational earth-centered conviviality when grace seeps through every fiber of our being, and for the greater part we get it right.

The closer we look at our long evolutionary story and contemplate our creative breakthroughs—in stone-tool technology (now dated back to 3.3 million years), language, ritual making, art, music, dance, etc. (cf. Stout 2016)—the more it is becoming increasingly clear that we are not primitive savages, poisoned forever with the contagion of original sin. No, we are first and foremost beneficiaries of a dynamically gracious God who forever showers upon us original grace and abundant blessings. Is it not about time we began to live out our ancestral grace and become the cocreative beings our God wishes us to be?

One aspect of our incarnational, human condition still creates hurdles almost too daunting to negotiate, presenting all the religions with challenges that are not well handled. I refer to the contemporary exploration of human gender and the many complex questions associated with psychosexual growth and development. We are in the midst of vast cultural upheaval in which the pursuit of gendered intimacy has taken on a life of its own, transgressing cultural, ethical, and religious boundaries. No book on Incarnation today would be complete without attempting to discern what is transpiring in this intriguing and complex landscape.

Chapter 7

Sex and Gender:
New Incarnational Horizons

A society that believes that the body is somehow diseased, painful, sinful, or wrong is going to create social institutions that wreck destruction on the body of the earth itself.

—Paula Gunn Allen

In our society sex is wounded by a deep seated masochism which finds distorted satisfaction in the suppression of desire.

—Thomas Moore

A reviewer of this book might wonder why I am including a chapter on contentious issues such as gender and sex. It is widely assumed that elders have little interest in such matters, since they are long past the child-bearing age, and the allurements so widely associated with the sexually active are assumed to be of little interest to them. As for my second envisaged group of readers, namely, spiritual seekers, we expect them, too, to transcend the distraction of sexual propaganda and devote their energies to

124

the loftier matters of spiritual growth and development. Such perceptions are loaded with cultural stereotypes that have long outgrown their relevance. But the cultural baggage is still around, what postcolonialists call the residue—in this case, an inherited sexual phenomenology that is likely to take several more decades to dispose of its destructive influence.

Throughout this book, I invite the reader to the enlarged view of the human species illuminated for us particularly by contemporary paleontology. We cannot hope to do either cultural or theological justice to our species by clinging to our conventional anthropology, specifically the overbiologized identity of classical Greek times. We must outgrow our narrow anthropocentric boundaries, and for that to happen we must dispose of several inherited prejudices, particularly those cherished by the so-called Enlightenment (1650–1780).

In a landmark article in 1964, the Chinese American anthropologist Francis L. K. Hsu condemned the liberal and extensive use of the term *primitive,* and challenged researchers of all disciplines to refrain from its further use. Not until 2007, however, did the British Association of Social Anthropologists formally adopt Hsu's challenge. This derogatory term is still liberally used in popular journalism, reinforcing the idea that civilization is a very recent attainment of the human species and that those who predate our civilized culture (dated to about 5000 BCE) should be viewed as substantially inferior to those of us formed and molded by the civilized standards of more recent times.

In terms of human sexuality, the primitive ideology is challenged strongly by coauthors Christopher Ryan and Cacilda Jethá in their controversial book, *Sex at Dawn* (2010). The authors claim that prior to the rise of Agriculture (about ten thousand years ago), our ancestors had lived a promiscuous lifestyle. Having multiple sexual partners was common and accepted in the environment of evolutionary adaptedness, characterized by mobile self-contained groups of hunter-gatherers, with an egalitarian lifestyle similar to that adopted by our chimp ancestors,

the bonobos. According to the book, sexual interactions strength-
ened the bond of trust in the groups; far from causing jealousy,
social equilibrium and reciprocal obligation were both reinforced
by playful sexual interactions.

As one might expect, the book received mixed reviews, with
a particularly negative evaluation from those adopting a Darwinian perspective (cf. Saxon 2012). Some commentators highlighted the fact that the views expressed are not entirely new and
have previously been highlighted by both anthropologists and
primatologists. While acknowledging the focus on sex, serving
the goal of creativity (and not just procreation), Ryan and Jethá
fail to acknowledge its central contribution to the evolution of
spirituality, a dimension I will return to presently, one I consider
to be of marked significance for the understanding of Incarnation
explored in the present work.

Gendering the Human

As indicated frequently in previous chapters, religion is particularly culpable for upholding and promoting a derogatory and
debilitating view of human sexuality, and in the case of Christianity, it is our adherence to classical Greek philosophy, specifically the ideas of Plato and Aristotle, that are at the root of the
problem. In terms of gender and sexuality, Greek thought asserts
unambiguously that the human species consists of two comple-
mentary poles: male and female. The two identities are broadly
understood as being biologically ingrained and determined by
God, the creator of the natural order. *Biological gender (sex)*
includes physical attributes such as external genitalia, sex chro-
mosomes, gonads, sex hormones, and internal reproductive structures. Psychological/social stereotypes follow logically: men are
supposed to be rational, assertive, tough, and focused on material
success; women are supposed to be more emotional, modest, ten-
der, and concerned with a nurturing quality of life. According to
that same philosophy, the male is superior in strength, wisdom,

and fertility; the woman provides the passive, receptive incubator to fertilize the male seed and assure the continuance of the human race.

Some scholars trace the emergence of these binary distinctions to the respective roles adopted by men and women in the wake of the Agricultural Revolution some ten thousand years ago. Alesina et al. (2013) provide a valuable overview of the research upholding this view. Paul Seabright (2012) notes that in the aftermath of agriculture, conflict and division between the sexes reached new heights, with women consistently relegated to subservient, functional roles, very different from the more egalitarian collaboration they had known in earlier epochs.

Despite the several advances in paleontology (study of human origins) outlined in Chapter 5, we don't seem to have surfaced any reliable evidence for the delineation of gender roles in our deep ancient past. Ethnographic evidence, based on current indigenous peoples, largely upholds the model of male superiority, influenced as they are (like the rest of us) by developments of more recent centuries. Despite the paucity of evidence, we must not jump to the kind of conclusions that prevailed in the social sciences till the mid-twentieth century—and still find support in several religious groups—namely, that our ancient ancestors up till a few hundred years ago, simply did not have the intelligence for gender differentiation and viewed human sexuality as a biological propensity for human reproduction, as exemplified in animal behavior.

The World Health Organization defines gender in terms of socially constructed roles, behaviors, activities, and attributes that a given society considers appropriate for men and women. Since the mid-twentieth century, the biological determining of gender has been consistently challenged, ensuing at the present time with several theorists favoring a *socially constructed* view. Judith Butler (1990, 2004) is a frequently cited authority on this matter. She contends that being female is not *natural* and that it appears natural only through repeated performances of gender; these performances, in turn, reproduce and define the traditional categories of sex and/or gender. In other words, how we experience ourselves as male or female is largely the result of learned conditioning. The fact that males and females are corporeally constituted with different biological features is not being doubted; such characteristics are viewed as secondary to our identity.

Modern scholars, such as Frances E. Mascia-Lees (2009) and Anne Fausto-Sterling (2012), criticize the standard binaries of sex and gender, arguing that both are fluid concepts that exist along a spectrum rather than as fixed binaries determined by biology or genetic imprinting. Gender tends to be viewed in terms of physical or physiological differences between male, female, and intersex bodies, including both primary sex characteristics (the reproductive system) and secondary characteristics (such as breasts and facial hair). It is this overt, common-sense perception that meets with increasing resistance, and as the grip on the monolithic understanding loosens, more people begin to experience inner shifts in their self-understanding. The increased frequency, and greater invisibility, of transgendered people is merely one outcome of this cultural transition.

Jeffrey John Kripal (2001, 17), in his controversial, cross-cultural research into erotic dimensions of male mysticism, presents the contemporary challenge in these words:

> As we now know from innumerable studies, physical genitalia, gender identity, gender role, and object choice are all potentially independent variables that can be combined in any number of ways, as the history of mysticism, with its stunning array of same-sex communities, male brides, symbolic and real eunuchs, gender transformations, cross-dressing saints, androgynes, hermaphrodites, and other third genders so powerfully demonstrates. . . . we should speak of gender as a sociocultural construct that is a matter of semiology rather than physiology.

Religions, and churches, hold huge resistance to this evolutionary development. For so long we have held the view that God creates everybody in their given biological identity, that there is a natural order, sometimes named as the natural law,[1] sanctioned by divine wisdom once and forever. Any suggestion of gender fluidity or plasticity is considered a pernicious denial of the laws of God inscribed in the human heart.

A critical factor here is the understanding of the human person adopted in classical Greek times and supported by a range of subsequent philosophers, of both secular and religious persuasion. In the previous chapter, I highlighted some key features of Aristotle's anthropology, which describes the human being as superior to all other life-forms: while plants, animals, and humans all have nutritive soul faculties, and animals and humans are endowed with sensitive soul faculties, only humans possess a rational soul. For Aristotle, rationality is the criterion that distinguishes humans from all other organic creatures.

One outcome of such rationality was the binary pairing we perceive throughout the natural world: earth v. heaven, body v. soul, matter v. spirit, male v. female. For Aristotle, the male possessed a superior form of rationality, so distinctive that Aristotle ended up describing the female as a misbegotten male. Authentic human nature belonged to the procreative power of the male seed (semen); the woman provided the fertile soil for the cultivation

---

[1] In its philosophical and theological usage, natural law has nothing to do with the laws of nature. Originally developed by Plato and Aristotle, and strongly endorsed by St. Thomas Aquinas, natural law claims that standards of morality are in some sense derived from, or entailed by, the nature of the world and the nature of human beings. St. Thomas Aquinas, for example, identifies the rational nature of human beings as that which defines moral law: "the rule and measure of human acts is the reason, which is the first principle of human acts" (Aquinas, ST I-II, Q.90, A.I). Accordingly, since human beings are by nature rational beings, it is morally appropriate that they should behave in a way that conforms to their rational nature. Thus, Aquinas derives the moral law from the nature of human beings as rational creatures (thus, *natural law*).

of that seed. Thus are laid the anthropological foundations that would define human nature for the next two thousand years, with Christianity particularly giving it the fullest possible reinforcement. Even the humanity of the historical Jesus was subjected to Aristotelian definition.

Biologically Determined Sexuality

From the above observations, human sexuality is defined as a biological capacity for the procreation of human life. It is a biological imperative, existing solely for one purpose, namely, human reproduction. And it belongs primarily to the male, in which sexual potential is invested, primarily in the male seed. Strictly speaking, the woman provides nothing of the power-filled potential, other than the fertile soil for the incubation and development of the seed. The ensuing sexual morality considered all other forms of sexual expression to be contrary to nature and sinful in the eyes of God. And since procreation was the primary goal, any suggestion of pleasure or human fulfillment from sexual intimacy was considered an aberration.

From a Catholic perspective it is worthy of note that marriage was not elevated to the status of a sacrament till the Council of Trent in the sixteenth century.[2] Going back to the time of the Roman Empire, most Christians were married in the same way as pagans, in common-law or *free* marriages. Christians were usually married in simple public ceremonies without any license or written agreement. Later on, after the reign of Christian Emperor Justinian (527–65), Christians were married in more formal civil ceremonies, according to the Justinian Code; though prayers and blessings were sometimes added to the ceremony, marriage was not a sacrament of the church, and it did not

---

[2] Cynthia Bourgeault (2010, 253, n5) makes an astute observation: "It took considerable theological manoeuvring to iron out the wrinkle of how something could be a sacrament that also involved carnal sin."

directly involve the church. The first known instance in the West of a blessing by a priest during a wedding ceremony is the 950 ritual of Durham, England. Although the fourth Lateran Council of 1215 required the blessing of a priest, it was unnecessary for the validity of the marriage. Only after the Council of Trent was a ceremony compulsory for Roman Catholics.

According to Trent, marriage is defined to serve a sole purpose: the procreation of the species. Catholics—and others—do not seem to have adverted to the blatant biological reductionism that was being invoked. Similarly, Catholics seem to have underrated the significant breakthrough in 1962 when the Catholic Church changed its definition of marriage, now declared to serve a double purpose: (1) the intimacy and love of the couple for each other and (2) the procreation of the species. It seems that the teaching authority of the Catholic Church in the early 1960s was well clued in to the major cultural shift taking place in our understanding of human sexuality and adjusted its teaching accordingly. Sadly, Catholicism, no more than any other major faith system, kept abreast of the evolutionary unfolding, as people on a universal scale sought (at least subconsciously) to transcend the biological condition and began to topple moral codes long regarded as indisputable.

By the late 1960s, psychosexual turmoil exploded on several fronts. As a social scientist, I consider this to be an evolution rather than a revolution. One could also describe it as a recapitulation, in which millions of people, unknowingly, were seeking to reclaim a more ancient understanding of human sexuality, primarily serving *creativity* (procreation being one small dimension) and *spirituality*, what the philosopher, Michel Foucault, called the *ars erotica*, which he claims has only existed in Ancient and Eastern societies. Free love became the order of the day, with an extensive breakdown in traditional monogamous commitment and an expanded set of sexual expressions, collated today under the synonym LGBTQ (Lesbian-Gay-Bisexual-Transgendered-Queer).

The ensuing evolution—like most major evolutionary shifts—was characterized by the paradoxical mix of breakdown and breakthrough. Sexual abuse flared on several fronts, often involving children, adolescents, and vulnerable adults. Sexual deviancy, promiscuity, and the extensive spread of pornography were deemed to be the primary culprits. Virtually nobody named—and still fail to do so—the explosion of sexual repression, buried deep in the human psyche over several previous centuries. It is the legacy of that *repression* that still continues to haunt our contemporaries, and particularly those of a religious background. Responsible incarnational redress will not be forthcoming till that deep psychic woundedness is acknowledged, named, and subjected to a more discerning and compassionate analysis.

Thus far, I am employing a postcolonial critique, briefly outlining the inherited cultural baggage through which we have long defined gender and sexuality. Millions have attempted to dislodge the baggage, some within the boundaries of church-controlled morality, but most by aggressively abandoning inherited wisdom, favoring, in many cases, a transgressive polymorphous free-for-all. Evolutionary transitions are never simple and typically a great deal more complex than those living through them are capable of recognizing. In the case of gender and sexuality, the creative alternatives would require a whole new anthropology, the dynamics of which are slowly evolving. The fuller emergence is likely to take several decades. Central to this new horizon is a shift from the inherited individualism toward a more relational paradigm in our understanding of human persons.

Toward a Relational Anthropology

Throughout the modern world, the Aristotelian definition of the human person dictates our social constructions of reality in politics, economics, education, science, and religion. There are meager residues of an alternative anthropology in some of our tribal cultures and among First Nations peoples. In Africa, one occasionally still hears allusions to the notion of *Ubuntu*: "I am because we are." Contemporary psychology occasionally seeks to reinstate this subverted view of the human with this cryptic assertion: "I am at all times the sum of my relationships and this is what gives me identity." Human identity is not merely a once-off accomplishment, but rather a life-long process unfolding over time and involving a complex range of influences, cosmic, planetary, organic, human, and spiritual. And let's add the Christian challenge, captivated succinctly by the late Walter Wink (2002, 157): "Incarnation is a task for us all to accomplish and not just some divine attribute of the historical Jesus."

Regarding the new relational paradigm, Albert Einstein captivated quite beautifully what is at stake in a remarkable letter written to a friend, grieving the loss of a loved one: "A human being is a part of the whole called by us universe, a part limited in time and space. He experiences himself, his thoughts and feelings as something separated from the rest, a kind of optical delusion of his consciousness. This delusion is a kind of prison for us, restricting us to our personal desires and to affection for a few persons nearest to us. Our task must be to free ourselves from this prison by widening our circle of compassion to embrace all living creatures and the whole of nature in its beauty" (quoted in Calaprice 2005, 206).

As indicated in our opening chapter, the Israeli/French psychoanalyst Bracha Ettinger (2006) is almost a lone voice in reclaiming an alternative anthropology, which situates the capacity for relationship as foundational to human flourishing, from the earliest stages of development in the mother's womb. That matrixial bond is the primal foundation that programs each human life for interconnection, interdependence, and cooperation, and not for separate individualism, propounded by Aristotle and so cherished by the patriarchal male whose view of life is often tainted by the allurement of separation, domination, competition, the key characteristics of what Lyons (2015) calls the *phallic culture.*

According to the relational understanding, none of us can grow into what the Christian gospel (Jn 10:10) calls the fullness of life, without being embedded in and sustained by a relational interconnectedness that spans the entire web of creation. There is no such thing as a lone individual. It is a distorted patriarchal fantasy that alienates and undermines our true nature. All of us are programmed for relationship, and it is through our relational interdependence that we fulfill our deepest dreams and contribute creatively to making the world a better place for all.

Relationality tends to be perceived as a capacity unique to humans pertaining particularly to human discourse articulated through friendship and various forms of intimacy and love. The very mention of intimacy in the culture of patriarchal management denotes sex, frequently viewed in the limited biological context outlined above. Most of the major religions embrace and endorse the inherited patriarchal norm of monogamous, heterosexual marriage as the primary, if not exclusive, context for the channeling and articulation of human sexual intimacy. Although not always explicitly stated, several other religious systems (e.g., Hinduism and Islam) follow the natural law theory, claiming that the primary purpose of human sexuality is that of the procreation of the species, and that is deemed to be only possible through the heterosexual expression of human sexuality. Some try to defend this conviction on the basis that sexual behavior among our immediate ancestors (the primates and higher animals) is primarily for reproductive purposes, a claim that is widely disputed in the scholarly research of recent times (cf. Roughgarden 2004).

In recent decades our understanding of human sexuality has undergone a social and cultural revolution, one that has been sensitively and comprehensively reviewed by the American ethicist Margaret A. Farley (2007, 23, 173):

> History remains silent regarding sexual exploitation, harassment, battery, and rape. Without attention to these unchanging experiences of women, there can be

no accurate analysis of sex and power, and indeed no real history of sexuality. . . . the meanings of sexuality are multiple—some creative, some destructive, some filled with love, some with the opposite of love. . . . At its most intense and most exhilarating heights, the experience of sex combines embodied love and desire, conversation and communication, openness to the other in the intimacy of embodied selves, transcendence into fuller selves, and even encounter with God.

For Farley, what we lack more than anything else is sexual justice, what she calls *just love*, the elements of which she elaborates at length. Central to her reflections is the double objective of separating sexuality from power and from biological conditioning. As the above quote indicates, sexuality signifies much more than human reproduction. Through its contemporary multiple expressions—heterosexual, homosexual, bisexual, transgendered (variously represented in the synonym LGBTQ)—humans seek to reincarnate a dimension of intimate meaning that has long been suppressed, and worse still, repressed. Thus today, we witness an explosion of wild eroticism with much free-wheeling *love making*, with at best a vague sense of boundary or conviction. Much of this behavior, I suggest, is repression exploding in our faces. Our heavy emphasis on sex for procreation has morphed into sex for recreation. It will take time to find a meaningful middle ground, the pursuit of sexual justice, and an ensuing empowering sense of intimacy, so well articulated by Margaret A. Farley.

In this brief overview, four key concepts require our focused attention, as these will be foundational to the evolving sense of Incarnation in the twenty-first century:

(1) *The Erotic.* The word is extensively used to denote salacious, instinctual energy, widely presumed to be the basis of the lurid pornography of our time, and the promiscuous behavior that leads to so much sexual acting-out. In its original meaning, the erotic denoted the capacity for deep bonding exemplified in the life of the holy divine itself (cf. Avis 1989;

Black 2003).[3] In other words, the erotic has long been recognized as a mystical energy, through which humans seek deep intimacy with the Holy One (best understood in *Trinitarian* terms). Prior to the Aristotelian biological reductionism (outlined above), sexuality was broadly understood as the experiential mode through which one engaged with the intimacy of the Godhead itself. Evidence for this prehistoric conviction surfaces in ancient Chinese and Indian art. Many Indian temples are ornate, not merely with scenes of copulation between male and female, but with several group orgiastic images that defy any sense of rational explanation. We are now so conditioned by the biological imperative that it is virtually impossible to reclaim this ancient primordial wisdom. Paradoxically, it is being reclaimed precisely amid the promiscuous culture of our time, where growing numbers of people—unknowingly for the greater part—are striving to carve out a new psychosexual way of being in the world.

(2) *Power*. Many commentators allude to the pioneering work of the French philosopher Michel Foucault (1926–84), outlined in three volumes, published between 1976 and 1984. Foucault is often associated with the repressive hypothesis that he claims arose in the seventeenth century when both state and church sought ever greater control of sexual behavior. Despite a range of criticisms leveled at his research, it is his alignment of sexuality with the urge to dominate and control that is widely regarded as an original and perceptive insight. Foucault argues that we need to develop an *analytics* of power through which we understand sex as a cultural phenomenon often used to domi-

---

[3] Pope Benedict XVI in his first encyclical, *Deus Caritas Est* (2005), nos. 3–7, acknowledged this ancient sacred meaning of Eros, going on however to attribute its corruption to the practice of temple prostitution. Had he read the valuable critique of sacred prostitution by Stephanie Lynn Budin (2008), he would have been better able to honor his desire to redeem the foundational meaning of the erotic as "a passion for connection, the enemy of dichotomy and disconnection" (Nelson 1992, 130).

nate and control, not just moral behavior, but most attempts that humans might use to declare personal independence, or suggest alternative social and political strategies to counter those of the mainstream culture. Beyond Foucault's interest in the sexual analytics of our patriarchal cultures, I would like to add the more subtle ecclesiastical attempts to control humans by inculcating sin, guilt, shame, and unworthiness, precisely in the sexual realm: keep people feeling guilty and unworthy, and it is much easier to control them. Paradoxically, it is this same sinister desire for control that is at the basis of a great deal of sexual abuse, within and outside the churches; in other words, sex abuse (in all its forms) is not so much about deviant sexuality, as about a raw repressed yearning for power and domination (see Jantzen 1995; Sipe 1995; Keenan 2011).

(3) *Woundedness and Repression.* Eugene Kennedy, one-time Catholic priest who later trained as a psychotherapist, wrote an insightful book on clerical celibacy, suggesting that many if not all priests bear an underlying sexual woundedness, itself a consequence of the abuse of power within the institutional church (Kennedy 2001). While this analysis reinforces the abuse of power highlighted above, my personal sense is that the woundedness is endemic to humanity at large. Despite the sexual *revolution* of the late twentieth century, millions still internalize guilt, shame, fear, and inferiority in terms of their sexual well-being. This deep wound I would attribute to centuries of sexualized repression. And while religion is one major source of this repression, there are earlier precedents that seem to be related to the commodification of the land in the wake of the Agricultural Revolution. Our human forced separation from the organic web of life, embedded in the land itself, seems to have distorted every erotic dimension of our being. No longer could we enjoy the convivial pleasure and bonding, our God-given inheritance as disciples of a Trinitarian, relational deity. Our erotic desiring was gradually disconnected from the encircling web of creation, and our capacity for embodiment became misplaced, and from

the ensuing confusion, our very souls were filled with pain and anguish, with the ensuing repression that haunts us even to the present time. A great deal of the rampant, widespread sexual abuse in our world (and not just in the church) needs to be understood afresh against this backdrop. Thomas Moore (1998, 243, 248) expresses well our enduring sexual anguish:

> We become inordinately absorbed in that which we neglect, and we display outlandishly what we do not deeply possess. This inversion of values, full of paradox, is a pattern that makes sense of our extreme interest in things and our tendency at the same time to treat things badly. . . . The principle at play is simple: whatever we don't have the imagination to weave into our human lives beautifully and intimately will haunt us in the form of autonomous temptations and shadow values.

(4) *The Sexual Spectrum.* It is generally assumed that monogamy evolved in the wake of the Agricultural Revolution in tandem with more genderized social streamlining and throughout the twentieth century won the unanimous support of all major religious systems. In several cultures, the monogamous partnership consists of a male and a female through whom sexual exchange is generally assumed to be a fixed biological inheritance. Several cultures have known other variations, notably, the calabai and calalai of Indonesia, two-spirit Native Americans, and the hijra of India—all represent more complex understandings of gender than allowed for by a simplistic binary configuration. And in recent decades, intersexed people have become much more visible in human society. This gradual undoing of the previous monolithic system, is giving way to a new sexual fluidity in which gender is often viewed as socially constructed, and sexual identity is capable of evolving into different articulations across a single lifetime. Consequently, homosexuality or bisexuality need not necessarily be the dualistic opposite of heterosexuality. Much of the contemporary rhetoric about sexual orientation may be

more of a cultural loosening up of past fixed identities, as we evolve into more polymorphous human beings. Claire Ainsworth (2015) provides a fine overview on the genetic research favoring the spectral understanding of sexual identity.

Psychosexual Education

The above observations depict a cultural landmine with daunting challenges for those responsible for child upbringing and education. Throughout much of the contemporary world, married adults often feel inhibited in speaking openly about sexual matters with their spouses or partners. Even within the intimacy of long-term monogamous relationships, human sexuality is not an easy subject for conversation. This further undermines the possibility of mature and empowering discourse with offspring, whether children or adolescents. In several Western countries, therefore, schools are expected to fill this formative vacuum, and sex education in schools rarely touches either the intimate or sacred depths of what is involved in sexual flourishing and development.

Human sexuality has long been shrouded in a felt need for respectful privacy, which all too often translates into a crippling toxic secrecy, inhibiting spouses from empowering conversations on respective loving and erotic needs, and undermining parental skill in passing on sexual wisdom to future generations. Inevitably, we end up in an ensuing cultural vacuum quickly filled in with our pornographic allurements and a great deal of salaciously addictive exploitation. There is an urgent and widespread need for responsible adult conversation on a subject that touches the lives of every person.

For a start, we need to shift our understanding of sexuality from its physiological base in genitality and our inherited biological conditioning, reducing sexuality to a process of procreation. Instead we need to revision sexuality as *the totality of our creative erotic energy, mediated through our feelings, moods, and emotions in all forms of human interaction.* In a word, it is our sexuality that defines our humanity as creatures programmed with the deep desire for intimate relating. Our sexuality is a psychic energy that we inherit from the universe itself, fueled by the desire to relate more deeply and intimately. Beneath and beyond the lofty aspirational language of love (cf. 1 Cor 13:1–13) is an energy of attraction and convergence that permeates every sphere of creation. In our embodied human condition it becomes the life force we call sexuality.

Another source that illuminates sexuality's deeper meaning is that intense realm of spiritual experience known as mysticism. Here I am following some of the seminal insights of religious philosopher Jeffrey John Kripal (2001, 17):

> One of my central contentions in reading the signs of this rich human sexual diversity is that mystical communities and literatures have offered some of the most successful, if still ethically ambiguous, venues in which alternative sexualities and genders have expressed themselves. . . . I thus read mystical texts, first and foremost, as cultural sites of sexual and gender liminality, as semiotic openings to a more polymorphous erotic existence that would be impossible within the more orthodox parameters of the social register in question. Whereas sexuality is canalized into heterosexual procreation within most societies, here, in the mystical texts it is freed, as it were, from such strictures and so is able to manifest itself in other, less "acceptable" ways. Among these the homoerotic certainly holds an important place.

This is quite a provocative claim, one that several scholars of mysticism are likely to take issue with, despite substantial evidence furnished by Kripal and the sources he cites.[4] Such a

---

[4] Kripal's primary research interest is that of male mysticism and the homoerotic dimension: "What I am suggesting is that Christian male erotic mysticism is inevitably homoerotic in doctrinal structure, and that this doc-

claim helps to make sense of the pre-Aristotelian understanding (alluded to earlier) that sexuality has long been understood in terms of creativity and spirituality. Although not stated in such explicit terms, that is clearly the view upheld by contemporary commentators such as Thomas Moore (2001), Anthony Giddens (1992), and Daniel T. Spencer (1996). How do we incorporate such insight and wisdom into a sexual educational strategy for the twenty-first century? And in terms of the present work, how do we integrate this understanding with an incarnational theology that can inform and illuminate the sexual yearnings and desires of our age?

Gender and Sexuality in Revelation

In this book I will not review what the Bible says about sexuality, material that has been extensively covered by other specialists, with Jennifer Wright Knust (2011) providing a valuable overview. When it comes to human sexuality, the Christian scriptures embody several assumptions that no longer stand up to scrutiny, even within the religious realm known as *revelation*. The Christian scriptures are inundated with patriarchal values of power and domination, and with Greek metaphysical concepts prioritizing the male gender and biologically determined sexuality. Throughout the Hebrew scriptures (Old Testament), the male prerogative, by sexual insemination and cultural domination, is visible throughout the sacred text. In the New Testament, sexuality seems to be a nonissue in the case of Jesus, leaving a discerning vacuum, the significance of which is well captured in these

---

trinal structure privileges a homosexual orientation, certainly in mystical textual expression and most likely in actual physiological response as well" (Kripal 2001, 72). A corresponding female perspective, equally erotic, but without a focus on sexual orientation, can be gleaned from Beverly Lanzetta's *Radical Wisdom* (2005), along with her *Path of the Heart* (2015), and from the writings of the British theologian, Lisa Isherwood (2006, 2013).

words from Rita N. Brock (1992, 28): "An element of Christology is lacking until we can allow ourselves to formulate images
of Jesus entering as deeply into the passion of his sexuality as
we have done regarding the passion of his suffering." And for St.
Paul, with the end of the world on the horizon, he advises that
sex should be left out of the equation completely.

For Christian theologians throughout much of the Christian
era, God is declared to be nonsexual (or asexual), a state that all
Christians should strive to achieve. Only in this way, can Christians reverse the curse of Adam, inherited from the angels who
rebelled in heaven, and after their expulsion landed on earth and
began propagating through sexual intercourse. Even for married
couples, sex has long been viewed as a necessary evil (as inti-
mated by St. Augustine). The logic seems to be that sexuality is
a kind of divine contamination, with Satan as the primary agent
driving sexual arousal, pleasure, desire, and nonprocreative sex.
And because of this sanctioned perverse understanding of sexuality, only the dominant male, who seems to retain some semblance
of the ruling God, can exercise sexual prerogative, thus becoming
the only one capable of authentic incarnational empowerment
(via sexual procreation).

Thus, we encounter the unjust gender distortions that feature
in all the major world religions, the Christian version of which
I am highlighting in this book. Not until the second half of the
twentieth century did scholars begin to address this distorted
gendered imbalance, and the discernment continues as we seek
to unearth and reclaim the deeper truth. These are among the
complex issues currently under review:

- The apostles and disciples in the time of Jesus seem to
  have constituted a range of male and female members.
  A discipleship of equals (for which Elizabeth Schussler-
  Fiorenza is a leading voice) may be stretching too far the
  range of possibilities, but there seems to be little doubt
  that discipleship during the lifetime of Jesus himself

included several women, many of whom played roles every bit as significant as that of the twelve apostles.

- The gospels suggest that none of the twelve were on the hill of Calvary at Jesus's crucifixion; they had all fled, lest they too be crucified. Those same gospels state explicitly (even by name) that Mary Magdalene and other women were present, and it seems increasingly likely that it is that same Magdalene-led group that first witnessed the Resurrection and became the original foundation of the infant church.

- Fifty days later, at the event of Pentecost as recorded in Acts 2:1–11, the reconstituted group of twelve are gathered for this special event, and there is no reference to any women except for Mary the mother of Jesus. As I highlight in a previous work (O'Murchu 2015), it is highly unlikely that the twelve returned—apart from Peter, we never again hear of any of them. Luke needs them back to create a solid apostolic foundation for his two great heroes, Peter and Paul. And why put Mary in their midst? A token replacement for the real women apostles that he has chosen to make totally invisible?

- Despite the cruel invisibility to which these early female apostles have been subjected, scholars are beginning to piece together, not merely a broken, but a defaced, jigsaw. Although not frequently mentioned, it does appear that women played a number of crucial roles in the Pauline Churches, some on their own, more as husband and wife pairs, like Prisca and Aquila (Rom 16:3; 1 Cor 16:19), Andronicus and Junia (Rom 16:7), Philogus and Julia (Rom 16:15), along with female pair collaborators such as Euodia and Syntyche (Phil 4:2–3) and Tryphaena and Tryphosa (Rom 16:12). The woman, Phoebe, named in Romans 16:1 as a deaconess, was the one who was entrusted to bring the letter of the Romans to Rome. In this capacity, she was not a mere postal mistress. She would have had to read the letter publicly to various groups in Rome, some quite learned; she would have preached and explained its contents and dealt with several questions that audiences would have surfaced. In a culture where it has long been assumed that women were domestic, backroom servants, and often treated like slaves, does Phoebe represent another female configuration too long ignored, that of a remarkably intelligent, competent woman, entrusted with many of the hefty responsibilities of Christian witness and proclamation? It leaves us with the burning question: was she an exception, or were there more—perhaps hundreds—like her? Contemporary scholarship suggests that extensive female apostolic involvement was very much to the fore.

- In a comprehensive scholarly study, Carolyn Osiek and Margaret MacDonald (2006) highlight the significance of house-churches in early Christianity, up to an estimated two hundred years before formal churches were created. From this home/family base, women seem to have played a major role in the development and spread of early Christianity. While the male hierarchical church adopts the temple and synagogue as foundational structures, the more organic evolution of Christian faith and praxis was probably a much more egalitarian enterprise with women as catalysts and leaders in the newly emerging faith system, based primarily in the family home, and known later as the house-church.

- Already by the end of the first Christian century, a new misogynist wave began to arise, the causes of which nobody has yet been able to identify. In fact Mary T. Malone (2014) indicates that it began as early as the 50–60 decade of the first Christian century, a fact we detect from the derogatory portrayal of women in the Letter to Timothy (see Tamez 2007). This gradual eclipsing of women's participative and empowering roles, not merely undermined the significance of women's contribution (particularly in the house-churches), but it began to deflect attention from women's unique witness to the gospel's Companionship of Empowerment.

The growing body of research into women's role in early Christianity indicates that women continued to participate in the life of the church, and the development of the faith, up till the fourth century when Constantine changed the whole tenor of early Christendom by adopting Christianity as the official religion of the Roman Empire. From there on, patriarchal males dominate the landscape, progressively obfuscating women's contribution and condemning them to ecclesial invisibility. Of course, women never ceased in their dedicated and devoted service to the gospel, and thanks to the more thorough and justice-based research of our time, we are beginning to redress the oppressive gender and sexual imbalances that have haunted our incarnational faith for far too long.

A New Incarnational Horizon

Some readers will wonder why I chose to include much of the controversial material of this chapter, particularly since it is so contested and opposed by Christian churches. I am attempting to be as faithful as possible to Christianity's nonnegotiable priority: seek *first* the New Reign of God (Matt 6:33), the gospel's Companionship of Empowerment, within which the values of empowerment, inclusivity, and justice must never be compromised.

Addressing the issue of gender, and seeking to redress our inherited historical and cultural distortions, is a movement that has already gained substantial momentum on a universal scale. I believe this is a movement of the Spirit, despite the fact that some religions still consider it a postmodern aberration. From a Catholic perspective, I am not concerned merely with women's ordination; as I pen these words, a debate is going on in the Catholic Church about the wisdom of ordaining women as deacons, a development I consider to be a gross distraction from the more substantial issues I raise in this book. Striving to make clericalism more inclusive, will do little, if anything, to make Christianity a more empowering and liberating faith for the twenty-first century. My primary interest is the nonclerical sphere, not the clerical domain.

The contemporary discourse on human sexuality creates a range of negative reactions from all major world religions. From a sociological perspective, it feels like the last bastion that the religions feel they must salvage and protect. Despite the biological conditioning that millions of contemporary human beings are questioning (and rejecting), the religions still seem to regard this psychosexual foundation as a God-given endowment that must never be questioned. Religionists seem to be largely unaware of the recent historical emergence of this biologically based understanding of human sexuality. We are dealing with a phenomenon certainly no more than ten thousand years old (within a human evolutionary story of an estimated *seven million* years), probably far less than that. We have embraced and acculturated a sense of human sexuality that is mechanistic, functional, and grossly anti-incarnational.

An attempt at a more wholesome understanding of Incarnation, and particularly one that honors the priority of the new Companionship of Empowerment, must strive to integrate a more empowering and liberating understanding of human sexuality. Of course, that does not mean going along with every fad and fancy of our contemporary highly sexualized culture. With discerning hearts, however, we need to ask, why has sexuality become so reckless, promiscuous, and pornographic? Are we witnessing a rebellion against well-established cultural/religious values? *Or against a repression of festering wounds that humans are no longer prepared to tolerate?* My sense is, that it is the latter, not the former.

An incarnational theology for the twenty-first century must not dodge the complex and urgent psychosexual issues of our age. We must enter into a deeper, more discerning conversation on a phenomenon that touches the core of our God-given humanity, and that core is carrying the pain and woundedness of many centuries. Without healing, and a culture where sexuality can be talked about in more adult, empowering ways, the incarnational significance of every faith remains seriously debilitated.

We have long sought such healing through the Christian notion of redemption and the long-held allurement of the Cross of Jesus as the symbol for liberation and salvation. Of all the issues in our inherited Christianity that have undermined incarnational flourishing, this might well be the most deviant. By isolating the *death* and Resurrection of Jesus, and inflating their importance, we have seriously undermined and distorted the saving and empowering significance of the *life* of Jesus. The rebalancing so urgently needed is the subject of our next chapter.

Chapter 8

Redemption and
the Corruption of Incarnation

*Violence is what we get when we do not know what else
to do with our suffering.*

—Parker Palmer

*We need to address suffering in a way that gives us a
moral imperative to seek its amelioration, not reconcile
us with it.*

—Elizabeth Johnson

God came in the body, in the human life of Jesus! That has been,
and continues to be, the foundational meaning of Christian
Incarnation. But with one important qualification: *it is above all
else a tortured body on a Roman Cross.* Down through the ages,
it is the crucified Jesus more than any other iconic image that has
sustained and inspired Christian faith.

For millions of poor and oppressed people, the Cross continues to be a symbol of love, hope, consolation, and reassurance. And in the wider human population, even rich and wealthy
people revere the Cross and draw comfort from it in times of
doubt and anguish. There is another dimension to such devotion,

which has lost much of its impact in recent decades, namely, the conviction that suffering is good for the soul, that holy people will always suffer, and that our sufferings accrue merit for salvation in a life hereafter.

For much of Christian history, the Cross and the emphasis on suffering served a range of purposes that today are seen as a serious betrayal of Christian Incarnation. Over several centuries, the martyrs were hailed as outstanding witnesses of incarnational embodiment, a view that has been fundamentally challenged by scholars such as Candida Moss (2013). The salvific value of suffering also dominates our inherited views of the ancient desert ascetics, and once again this conviction has been seriously challenged by the monastic scholar James Goehring (1999) among others. This antibody rhetoric, with the emphasis on asceticism, punishment, deprivation, and denial of legitimate desire, has had a devastating impact on women's bodies particularly, long regarded as seductive and prone to hysteria, deemed to be seriously defective compared to the prowess and integrity of the male form.

In short, the more the human body could be conformed to the suffering body of Christ on the Cross, the better one's chances of being authentically holy, with a greater possibility of obtaining salvation in a life hereafter. Throughout the latter half of the twentieth century, the emphasis swung significantly as theologians shifted the focus to the Resurrection rather than the crucifixion of Jesus. Calvary and the Cross are merely one aspect of the incarnational breakthrough, and it must always be seen as the prerequisite for the enduring hope encapsulated in the event of the Resurrection. In the words of St. Paul, "And if Christ has not been raised, our preaching is useless and so is your faith" (1 Cor 15:14).

Unraveling the Myth of Suffering

The primary purpose of this book is to reclaim and expand our understanding of Incarnation. We face an awesome challenge in terms of the material of the present chapter, which basically wrestles with the role of pain and suffering in an incarnational faith for the twenty-first century. A great deal of clutter needs to be cleared away, particularly the following ideological (postcolonial) views that have long remained covert and are influential even to our own time:

- Suffering is good for the soul.
- Suffering keeps us humble and obedient.
- Suffering is a great remedy for sin.
- Suffering enhances our chances of salvation hereafter.
- Suffering is inevitable in a world contaminated by original sin.
- Christ suffered, and so must we.
- The just suffer in this life; the wicked suffer in the life hereafter.
- Suffering creates codependency on superior powers (medical, social, religious) and therefore is covertly encouraged in patriarchal cultures.
- Suffering keeps people feeling weak and unworthy, and therefore it is much easier to control their behavior.
- Suffering is a divine prerogative that cannot be understood apart from active faith.
- Suffering is a mystery and is not really a problem for those with strong faith.
- In the death and Resurrection of Jesus, suffering (and death) has been upended.

There is a mystique about suffering that inhibits most people from looking too closely. One could say of suffering what Terry Eagleton (2010, 65) says of evil: "it is a transcendence gone awry. Perhaps it is the only form of transcendence left in a post-religious world. We know nothing anymore of choirs of heavenly hosts, but we know about Auschwitz." The contemporary reader can add Cambodia's Pol Pot, Rwanda, ISIS, etc. For most people, it is too frightening and depressing to even look at the violence and barbarity of our time. And those that do—philosophers and theologians—often provide analyses that sound unreal and far-fetched to many reflective adults in the contemporary world.

In keeping with the expansive view explored in this book, I want to suggest that our problem with suffering (and what is often described as *evil in the world*) is too narrow and anthropocentric. We are so preoccupied with human suffering that we miss what is staring us in the face: *suffering is ubiquitous, and clearly serves some important evolutionary purpose.* If we get rid of it, we are basically seeking to eradicate life itself, with its paradoxical meaning and purpose. When human suffering becomes wrapped up in theories of redemption and salvation—and every religion has one or another variant—then the anthropocentric focus becomes so narrowly exclusive that we end up reinforcing the very dilemma we are seeking to resolve. We actually enhance the very meaninglessness of the suffering we are striving to eradicate.

The Great Paradox

Modern technology promises us a world where one day human aging will be arrested, disease and death will cease to exist, and the perfect machine will bring an end to human struggle and drudgery. It is a delusory myth that strongly appeals to scientific futurists of our time. Christianity has its own version of this utopian myth: the lamb and the lion will lie down together (Is 11:6). And all the nasty stuff will somehow be changed and transformed. Have no fear; *it is never going to happen.* And if perchance it ever did, it would be the greatest apocalyptic disaster creation would ever know.

Creation cannot survive, and less so thrive, without its dark side. There is a quality of destruction, decay, and death that is essential to creation's flourishing. Without this downside there can never be evolutionary breakthroughs. And the consequence of this destructive dimension is what we call evil, pain, and suffering. Obviously, I am not suggesting fatalistic acquiescence.

Indeed, I am arguing a case for the very opposite: an enduring sense of hope, which it seems to me is not possible without first coming to terms with what I will henceforth describe as the *great paradox*. It is usually described as the paradox of *creation-cum-destruction* (with both concepts carrying equal weight), otherwise named as *the unfolding cycle of birth–death–rebirth*. And it transpires all over creation, on the macro and micro scales alike.

Is this how God created the world? It seems so, to which the average religionist is likely to retort, "How could anyone believe in such a capricious God?" But who is actually capricious, God or us? Many of us have been heavily indoctrinated by the classical Greek notion of the perfect, omniscient (all-knowing), omnipotent (all-powerful), transcendent (totally independent of all else), immutable (never changing), impassible (beyond suffering), eternal God, the one who rules and controls everything. Most people don't seem to realize that these divine attributes are actually projections of a human species seeking absolute control over everything. The all-powerful deity is actually a projection of power-hungry humans. Such an understanding of God is little more than five thousand years old and is significantly different from how we related with Holy Mystery for most of our evolutionary story of some seven million years.

Our ancient ancestors had a very different understanding of the divine life force. Because of their closeness to the natural world, the ancients, somewhat like contemporary indigenous (tribal) peoples, knew a convivial relationship with the living universe, experiencing the daily interaction of life and death, creation and destruction, without—it seems—our contemporary compulsion for domination and control. What, to many of our contemporaries, seems like a baffling paradox (creation-cum-destruction) was known to our ancestors thousands of years before Greek metaphysics and patriarchal domination wrecked the whole perceptual edifice. And this earth-centered affiliation was not some type of infantile enmeshment, as the Greeks suggested. It was a quality of engagement, the deeper meaning of which seems to have eluded the patriarchal worldview of recent millennia.

We need to recover this long lost incarnational wisdom. It knows how to tolerate confusion and contradiction without being overwhelmed by either. It knows how to respect the evolutionary trajectory of every embodied form, human and planetary alike, in a process that is complex, unpredictable, fluid, chaotic (as in chaos theory), and often downright baffling. And for our ancient ancestors it was not just a matter of getting it right or wrong (in all probability, dualistic splitting was unknown at that time). It was more a question of befriending the unfolding process, trusting its evolutionary momentum. The good and bad were two sides of the one coin; both were necessary for life's flourishing.

The key word here is *paradox*, which may be described as *a contradiction with meaning written underneath*. On the surface, it makes little or no sense. Only the discerning eye (or heart) can perceive the underlying meaning. A familiar example occurs in the writings of St. Paul (cf. 2 Cor 12:9–11): "When I am weak then I am strong." At a rational level, the statement makes no sense, yet many among us can recall life experiences within which the statement rings true. It is the mystic more than anybody else who can entertain and embrace this paradoxical wisdom. Consider this description from the theologian Leonardo Boff (1995, 161–62, 70):

> Mysticism is life apprehended in its radicalism and extreme density. Existence is endowed with gravity, buoyancy, and depth when this is conceived and known appropriately. Mysticism always leads to the transcendence of all limits. It persuades us to examine other aspects of things than those we know and to suspect that reality is more than a mere structure concealing the realm of the absurd and the abyss, which can strike fear and anguish into our hearts. . . . The mystic is not

detached from history but committed to it as transformation, starting from a nucleus of transcendent meaning and a minimal utopian dimension which, in as much as it is religious, enables the mystic to be more perceptive than anybody else.

This alternative consciousness, with its capacity for deeper perception and understanding, is not merely an endowment of the human mystic; more controversially, it constitutes the underlying wisdom through which creation itself evolves and flourishes, as illustrated by the Australian theologian Anthony J. Kelly (2015). On the planetary scale, earthquakes serve as a good example. Metaphorically, an earthquake can be described as the earth-body releasing its pent-up energies, so that it can continue to grow and flourish in a more creative way. Without earthquakes, we would have no earth, nor would any of us be around even to speculate on this baffling paradox of birth–death–rebirth.

So, does God will the death of 240 thousand innocent people, as happened in Pakistan in 2005, or of wholesale environmental catastrophe resulting from the 2004 Asian Tsunami? There is no logical or rational answer to this question because we are engaging a form of wisdom that is beyond rationality. Worthy of note however is the fact at an 8.0 earthquake (Richter scale) in the island of Guam in 1991 resulted in no human casualties, while that of Pakistan (7.4 on the Richter scale) led to 240,000 deaths. When we note that the island of Guam is a territory of the United States, with all the buildings of an earthquake-resistance quality, and there are no such buildings in Pakistan (because the poor country can't afford them), we begin to see a way through the paradox. It quickly becomes obvious that the problem is not with the earthquake, nor with God, but with the avaricious humans who choose not to share resources equally and justly across the human population.

It is not God or the earthquake that killed 240,000 people in Pakistan. It is fellow humans who caused the slaughter, addicted to the unjust distribution of earthly and human resources. We know how to cope with the earthquake in the case of Gaum in 1991. We could do so universally if we were committed to justice and equality all round.

Admittedly, we cannot always find a meaningful or reasonable explanation for those freaks of nature that wreak havoc on nonhuman life-forms. When dealing with paradox, there will always be untidy elements that transcend rational explanation. But even in such situations we need to press the human dimension. In August 2005, hurricane Katrina wreaked havoc on the city of New Orleans as did superstorm Sandy along the east coast of United States in October 2012.

Nothing to do with humans, we are quick to retort! A capricious act of God, others suggest! In the wake of Katrina, commentators noted that hurricanes seem to come with a much greater ferocity than previously recorded. Other environmentally related factors, for example, global warming, may be a contributory factor, which immediately raises suspicion of a human contribution as we slowly but gradually realize that indirect human interference, reinforcing a range of ecological imbalances, may well be a critical factor in several major natural catastrophes.

While we cannot be certain about the human role in natural catastrophes, it is becoming increasingly clear that human behavior contributes significantly to many forms of human suffering on our earth. The evil we seek to impute elsewhere, to Satan, or the Devil, may well be a deluded projection that arises from our own wrong interference in the scheme of things. At the very least, we need to come to terms with our appalling ignorance of the paradoxical world we inhabit—within and without. Only when we become aware of the great paradox will we gradually begin to realize that most of the meaningless suffering within and around us *is actually caused by humans*, not by God or by natural catastrophes. It is our ignorance of the great paradox, and our inability (or unwillingness) to engage it proactively that is at the root of most, if not all, the meaningless suffering in the world.

The language of paradox is written all over creation. It is there for us to read and discern. When we do attend to it, it seems to make life more tolerable, bearable: dare I suggest, more meaningful. When we fail to attend, we expose ourselves to forces that can be cruel and devastating. Apparently, we do have a choice. The big problem, however, is that the choice seems to lead in directions that are alien to our imperial Western consciousness, to our rational ways of perceiving and acting, and to our prized sense of being in control of the contingent nature of the world we inhabit. To opt for the other choice—follow the *stupid* indigenous peoples—defies our intelligence and common sense. It feels like betraying or abandoning all we have worked so hard for, all that constitutes the very foundations of a civilized world.

The Meaning of Suffering

The perennial question, therefore, relates to the suffering we humans cause and exacerbate, because, apparently, we have lacked the wisdom to read the great paradoxes of life in a more enlightened way. A universe without pain and suffering is simply impossible. Suffering in itself is endemic to every incarnational embodied form. Suffering is not the problem; it is our faulty perceptions that cause the problem. It is WE who need to change, not the messy world that has been messed up in the first place by our reckless interference. The British philosopher, Terry Eagleton, captures well the underlying confusion when he writes, "There is a diabolic delight to be reaped from the notion of absolute destruction. Flaws, loose ends, and rough approximations are what evil cannot endure. This is one reason why it has a natural affinity with the bureaucratic mind. Goodness by contrast, is in love with the dappled, unfinished nature of things." (2010, 101).

Eagleton goes on to make a second crucial observation about the meaningless suffering that surrounds us on a daily basis. Contrary to the claim that the fundamental flaw of original sin is a major contributory factor, Eagleton writes, "The point is that most wickedness is institutional. It is the result of vested interests and anonymous processes, not of the malign acts of individuals" (2010, 143). I would like to add that it is the corruption and usurpation of power within all our major institutions that cause most, if not all, the meaningless suffering in the modern world.

The insidious nature of human angst and misery is partly due to the Christian notion of atonement. First introduced in the Middle Ages, mainly by St. Anselm, the basic argument goes like this: God was angry with humankind's waywardness (sin), and like a feudal Lord, God demanded that satisfaction and reparation should be made. And he chose (or persuaded) his son, Jesus, to be the necessary scapegoat. Jesus paid the penalty of humanity's sin, bringing forgiveness, imputing righteousness, and reconciling us all to God. According to this view, Jesus's death paid the penalty for sin, and through our faith we can now accept Christ's substitution as payment for all human sinning. Some scholars, such as Gustav Aulen in his book *Christus Victor,* goes on to broaden the theory claiming that in the death and Resurrection of Jesus, sin, death, and evil have been overcome—forever!

While contemporary scholars try to claim that there is really no biblical basis for Atonement theory, there are a number of Old Testament allusions (e.g., Yom Kippur—Lv 16:1–34 and 23:26–32; Nm 29:7–11), and some key statements from St. Paul, that seem to have an unambiguous meaning: "For our sake he made him to be sin who knew no sin, so that in him we might become the righteousness of God" (2 Cor 5:21); "Christ redeemed us from the curse of the law by becoming a curse for us —for it is written, *Cursed is everyone who is hanged on a tree*" (Gal 3:13).

Fundamentalist and evangelical Christian scholars still cling to the theory, acknowledging that humans are irredeemably perverted (sinful) and cannot be healed (saved) except through an act of divine intervention, which they claim happened, once and for all, through the death and Resurrection of Jesus. Interestingly, Yale theologian Miroslav Volf, hardly a conservative evangelical, argues that "the only way in which non-violence and forgiveness will be possible in a world of violence is through displacement or *transference* of violence, not through its complete relinquishment" (Volf 1996, 302).

In the closing decades of the twentieth century, several Christian scholars highlighted the flawed nature of Atonement theory itself (see the valuable overview in Pugh 2015). The French theorist, Rene Girard, claims that penal substitution is an inherently *violent* model of the atonement and has achieved little other than reinforcing the very violence it seeks to eradicate. Several feminist theologians view Atonement theory as a form of *divine child abuse*, one that has contributed significantly to the victimization of women in particular. Black liberation theologian James Cone links the model to defenses of slavery and colonialism, while British ethicist Michael Northcott suggests that it is no coincidence that leaders of the Religious Right, for whom the model is so central, are such staunch advocates of the *lex talionis*, capital punishment, and the war on terror.

The Christian emphasis on atonement—describing Jesus as the lamb of God who takes away the sins of the world—seems to be rooted in the feast of Yom Kippur in the Hebrew scriptures (described in the book of Leviticus, chapters 16 and 23). John Shelby Spong (2007, 2016) persuasively argues that it is our Gentile-inherited tendency to literalize events like Yom Kippur—frequently distorting the original Jewish context—that leaves us with a grossly convoluted understanding of atonement—in both the Old Testament setting and in its application to the death of Jesus. In the present work, I will not engage with the complex intricacies of Atonement theory, summarized for the average reader in Ben Pugh's (2015) valuable overview. Instead I wish to move on to the more expansive issues, congruent with the extended analysis being explored in the present work. For adult faith seekers of our time, three urgent questions arise:

- Prior to the time of Jesus, what evidence are we using to indicate that humans lived in a tragic alienation from God? My studies in anthropology and paleontology suggest quite a different divine–human relationship. If we wish to retain the notion of original sin, I propose we locate its origins in the shadow side of the Agricultural Revolution (as done by Steve Taylor [2005]) and not at the beginning of human evolution.

- It seems to me that all the world religions, and specifically the monotheistic ones, indulge in a problematic anthropocentrism that requires urgent redress. It is an anthropology without an appropriate sense of context, pitted over against the wider web of creation, a dualistic split which increasingly makes no sense in our age.

- Related to my last point, it seems grossly irresponsible to lump together human sin, death, and Satan. Death is an integral dimension of all organic life-forms. Death is a God-given endowment, without which we cannot have new life. Death is not an evil to get rid of, but rather a central ingredient of the life force that needs to be understood in another light. We must stop demonizing death and instead learn to befriend it responsibly.

The Rhetoric of Sacrifice

One particular aspect of the Atonement theory requiring a more discerning scrutiny is that of sacrifice. The sacrifice of lambs played a central role in the faith of the Jews. In the Passover feast, one of the main Jewish holidays marking God's deliverance of the Israelites from bondage in Egypt, the slaying of the Passover lamb and the applying of the blood to doorposts of the houses (Ex 12:11–13), evoked the deliverance into new freedom and for the Jewish people a reintegration into their own land. Sacrificing lambs in the temple was a daily occurrence, a ritual to mark the forgiveness of sins. Both Jeremiah and Isaiah foretold the coming of One who would be brought "like a lamb led to the slaughter" (Jer 11:19; Is 53:7) and whose sufferings and sacrifice would provide redemption for Israel.

Understandably, then, the early Jewish-Christians would view the death of Jesus against this background, and we have long assumed that Jesus himself would have done the same. But this assumption loses credibility, at least on two fronts:

- According to Spong (2016, 206ff.) the celebration of Yom Kippur (and the accompanying ritual of sacrifice) was a symbol of human yearning for perfection and not about victimization to placate an angry God.
- If we take seriously the gospel strategy of the new empowering companionship (the Kingdom), we cannot avoid the inescapable truth that salvation and redemption (if we wish to retain such language), comes through the life of Jesus and not merely through his death. In fact, it is much more congruent to understand his death as the price paid for a life radically lived, an argument persuasively made by scripture scholar Stephen J. Patterson (2004, 2014), elaborated later in this chapter.

In this context, sacrifice indeed holds a central place. Its primary meaning from the original Latin is to *make something sacred* and not merely to give something up, as conventionally understood. However, the giving-up aspect is still significant, describing a sacrificial element visible throughout the entire creation. For example, every day the sun sacrifices tons of energy to make possible the process of photosynthesis through which the entire food chain is energized. Many species have to endure sacrifice, and some do so altruistically, for the sake of others; see the informative and inspiring overview of Bernd Heinrich (2013) and Norman Wirzba's valuable insights on sacrificial eating (2011, 110–43). In this sense sacrifice is a key element of empowering love.

According to John Dunnill (2013, 203), sacrifice is essentially about gifting: what do I have to give up or forgo for the benefit of another. It inculcates that spirit of generosity, so urgently needed in our consumerist age, addicted to acquisition, greed, and power. Dunnill views such generosity as a precondition for faith in God; I would rather emphasize its significance for a more incarnational understanding of the God who forever bestows upon creation the generous giftedness through which everything grows and flourishes.

But this deeper meaning has been overshadowed by the phenomenon of *scapegoating*, itself another central feature of Atonement theory (see the valuable elaboration in Girard [1986] and Campbell [2013]). It describes how a person or group is forced to carry blame for others or to suffer in their place. Derived from the Old Testament (Lev 16:8ff), a goat is let loose in the wilderness during Yom Kippur after the high priest symbolically laid the sins of the people on its head.[1] Jesus is clearly projected

---

[1] Sacrificial animal offerings have featured in several ancient religious practices; it is difficult to date the origin or development of such practices. W. Robertson Smith (in *The Religion of the Semites,* 2nd ed., London: Black, 1907), for example, traced the origins of sacrifice to a community's consumption of the totem animal in a festival meal, evidence for which cannot be reliably dated beyond 5000 BCE. He considered other kinds of sacrifice, including human sacrifice, to be corrupted forms of this original communion meal. Many other theorists have also emphasized the primacy of animal offerings, though in diverse ways. Thus, Edward Tylor's gift theory of sacrifice defined the offering of humans as a version of cannibalism, that is, as an alternative food offering to animal meat. Henri Hubert and Marcel Mauss based their sociological theory on the most complete descriptions of sacrificial rituals available to them: the animal offerings of the Vedic (Indian) and biblical (Jewish) traditions. Walter Burkert traced sacrifice back to the hunting of animals, Jonathan Z. Smith to the domestication of animals, and Marcel Detienne to the cooking of animals. Barbara Ehrenreich, combining elements drawn from Burkert and Bloch, suggested that the primordial experience of being hunted by large predators conditioned humans to accept the deaths of individuals for the sake of the larger community,

onto this role, even to the perverse level that the phenomenon of scapegoating becomes synonymous with sacralized violence. WE too easily forget that Jesus was killed because he posed a threat to Roman and Jewish imperialism, and not as a divine scapegoat sent to rescue sinful humanity.

It is the sacrifices that Jesus made in his lifetime—to bring about empowering and liberating justice—that require our discerning attention, not what happened merely in his death experience. In the words of Stephen J. Patterson (2004, 2), "One of the great mistakes of Christian theology has been our attempt to understand the death and resurrection of Jesus apart from his life. The first followers of Jesus generally did not do this.... His death and resurrection are directly related to his life; they issue from it." Jesus was killed because he was so empowering for the disillusioned, alienated people that the political and ecclesiastical systems of the day could tolerate him no longer and felt they had to get rid of him. He gave his followers no guarantee of heaven (nor of hell), but gave them a blueprint to recreate their own heaven here on earth (as in the parables and miracles).

Similarly, our adult commitment as Christian witnesses to empowering Incarnation in the twenty-first century. And when we remain focused on that primary undertaking, seek first the new companionship (cf. Matt 6:33), then not merely will we embrace our Christian faith at a deeper and more integrated level, but other long-neglected aspects of our sacred story as a human species assume renewed importance, both anthropologically and theologically.

---

a precarious condition ritualized both in sacrifice and in war. James G. Frazer collected a wide variety of rituals into a theory of sacrificial kingship in which the ritual sacrifice of kings undergirds most forms of traditional ritual, including the occasional sacrifice of human beings. Maurice Bloch argued that *rebounding violence* underlies not just sacrifices, but almost all religious and political rituals, and leads to the symbolic or actual domination of others through violence.

The Denial of Death

After evil and suffering, death is the next great enemy we would love to conquer. For St. Paul, death is the consequence of sin (Rom 6:23); it entered the world through the deviant behavior of the original human (Adam) (Rom 5:12). For St. Paul, and subsequent generations of Christians, the death and Resurrection of Jesus has "destroyed death forever" (1 Cor 15:26), and to that utopian hope, millions of Christians still adhere.

The great oriental religions of Hinduism and Buddhism take a very different approach, viewing death in reincarnational terms, whereby life and death are interwoven in an evolving recurring cycle, culminating in the release of the soul into the eventual fulfillment of Nirvana.

For most humans in the contemporary world, we dread death to the point where most of us refuse even to think about it, until life's circumstances compel us to do so, and then we either seek to escape the challenge or rationalize it as far as possible. Despite this widespread fear, we rub shoulders with death on a daily basis, and we remain largely unaffected by the deadly termination of life we mete out to fellow humans and to so many other species of our earth.

Our passive acceptance of the endless media coverage of carnage and atrocity betrays a love–hate relationship with death. We are simultaneously repelled by its terror and seduced by its mystique. The popular appeal of violent video games and Hollywood horror movies provides further proof of our morbid fascination with death. The overexposure to images and messages of death seems to have desensitized us to the terror of death and has made us more tolerant of violence and the random destruction of several life-forms.

In terms of the present work, I want to shift the focus, seeking to make the meaning of death congruent with the understanding of Incarnation that I am exploring. To that end I make the following key points:

- Death is an integral dimension of the great paradox of creation-cum-destruction, the recurring cyclic process of birth–death–rebirth. If we get rid of death, we have immediately terminated life as well.
- Death cannot be properly understood without a deeply integrated awareness and internalization of the great paradox described earlier in this chapter.
- Death is not a limitation, or an evil, in any sense. Death is a necessary good, an evolutionary, God-given imperative, for the development and flourishing of all life-forms.
- The negative preoccupation with death is largely the product of imperial patriarchal consciousness, the insatiable desire to conquer and control all life forces, to the deluded advantage of the patriarchs themselves.
- Monotheistic religions, heavily influenced by the patriarchal value system, reinforce the negative and problematic dimensions of death.
- The violent glamorization of death in public media is a perverse defense mechanism against the self-induced horror of death.
- Despite all the utopian hope of the various religions, most humans do not die with dignity nor with responsible love and care. Millions each year die anonymously and are not given a proper burial.

How do we get it right in regard to death? Where do we begin in the process of incarnational reintegration? Conventionally, for Christians, the Resurrection of Jesus is considered to be the breakthrough that strips death of its meaninglessness, an achievement wrought by Jesus and by nobody else. In its literal understanding, Jesus, unknown to anybody, and without any human assistance, came out of the grave and had bodily encounters with the apostles and others before ascending back to the heavenly realm outside this earth. Volumes have been written on this topic, long understood to be the greatest miracle of all in which Jesus himself overcame death and rose from the grave in a newly constituted body. In this approach, death and Resurrection always go together.

Throughout the second half of the twentieth century, Christian scholars raise doubts about this literal interpretation. For one thing, the three-tier cosmology makes no sense in our time. And when it comes to the Resurrection appearances recorded in the gospels, we need to remember the cultural context where spirit power was very real, and people had the capacity for mystical/visionary experiences long lost to our contemporaries. Recall the cryptic reminder from John Dominic Crossan (1996, 79): "My point, once again, is not that those ancient people told literal stories and we are now smart enough to take them symbolically, but that they told them symbolically and we are now dumb enough to take them literally." The gospel encounters with the risen Jesus may be more indicative of what was happening to the followers rather than what happened to Jesus himself. Literalists in the past used the empty tomb as *proof* for the Resurrection of Jesus, but those that continued to follow Jesus did not base their faith on the evidence of an empty tomb, but rather on the new awakening of God's living Spirit in their midst.

In other words, the power of the Resurrection is better discerned through the transformation wrought in the disillusioned followers of Jesus in the days and weeks after his tragic death rather than in what may have happened to Jesus himself. Instead of speculating on what actually happened to Jesus, let's ask what was the transformative power whereby the shattered, disillusioned disciples came back to a quality of faith upon which they staked everything from thereon, even to point of a martyr's death.[2]

---

[2] Most Christian readers will assume that I am referring to the male apostles (the twelve), but in fact those I have primarily in mind are the women disciples referred to in the Resurrection scene in all four gospels. As I indicate in a previous work (O'Murchu 2015), I believe these were the original disciples who laid the foundations of the Christian church, but our patriarchal misogynist history has virtually obliterated their foundational witness to the building up of the earliest Christian communities.

This links Resurrection with life rather than with death. It then becomes what Christian theology frequently asserts: *the fullness of life*. Therefore, Resurrection can be viewed as God's ultimate vindication that the life of Jesus (and not so much his death) was a life dedicated to transformative empowerment and extensive liberation.

Quantum physics helps to deepen our understanding of Resurrection (as explained above) while also illuminating the mystery of death—our own and that of the historical Jesus. All life-forms are constituted and sustained by living energy, that same life-force that enlivens everything in the creation around us. And it seems that energy needs to be embodied to function and flourish; without body, energy cannot do much. In the experience of my death—whatever the cause—the energy departs from my particular embodied configuration but does not evaporate into nothing. According to the basic laws of physics, energy is never wasted. Energy always reconnects with energy, to seek out a new embodied articulation, which is another way of understanding the enlivening power of Resurrection energy after the death of Jesus.

After my death, the energy of my embodied existence will go elsewhere. Exactly where, I don't know, and why do I need to know? Why not trust the universal cosmic wisdom within which energy is always recycled to cocreate even more complex organisms, human and otherwise? This reckless sense of trust in the benevolent nature of the universe—what Christians might call *Resurrection hope*—assumes additional meaning within the spirituality of indigenous peoples all over our planet, through their faith in the Great Spirit!

As I have explained in a previous work (O'Murchu 2012), belief in the Great Spirit has been observed in First Nations (tribal) peoples all over our earth, although most of these peoples have never actually encountered each other nor shared their unique spiritual wisdom. It flourishes ubiquitously, without bible, creed, church, or hierarchy. It is evidence of the energizing Spirit who for the indigenous peoples does not inhabit some distant heaven but is to be experientially encountered within the organic creation itself. For many such peoples, the dead are ancestors whose living spirit inhabits trees, mountains, lakes, etc. Primitive fiction or a quality of mystical wisdom our rational world cannot come to terms with? I will opt for the latter.

What I postulate in this explanation need not be in conflict with belief in an afterlife of heaven or hell. Rather it confronts us with the likelihood that we make our own heaven or hell, not in some distant transcendent realm, but right here in front of our eyes. The thousands of innocent children who die prematurely every day is hell on earth, and so is the butchery that results from warfare and violence. It is the pseudotranscendence we attach to death that makes it so tragic and frequently meaningless. We need to resolve the dilemma of death not in some transcendent afterlife, nor by projecting on to a divine scapegoat on a Cross, but right here upon the earth itself.

Both life and death are about the body, with its many incarnational dimensions explored in the present work. Life and death are both necessary for the energizing Spirit to become embodied in our world. Without that paradoxical mix, there is no life, nor mystery, nor meaning.

Healing the Split between Life and Death

As a species, we have been self-indoctrinated into a confused, functional, and codependent view of life. Most of the time, it seems, we miss its deeper meaning and purpose. And things are even worse when it comes to our understanding of death. Religion itself may well be the major culprit here. Organic life, throughout its entire universal span, thrives on the dynamic process of birth–death–rebirth, vividly illustrated by the former professor of biology at the University of Vermont, Bernd Heinrich, whose intensive study of creepy-crawly creatures, and their organic interdependence is entitled *Life Everlasting* (2013). Without this evolutionary process, life would become so clogged and stymied that many life-forms would rapidly disintegrate and self-destruct. The inbuilt decline, decay, and death we witness in the natural world is essential to the very well-being of all that lives.

Death, therefore, is not an evil in any sense. To the contrary, it is a precondition for all organic growth and development. The demonization of death seems to be largely a Christian invention, and one our human ancestors would never endorse. St. Paul claimed that death entered the world through the fault of one man (namely, Adam), and death is the consequence of sin. For Paul, the entire gospel is about the death and Resurrection of Jesus (cf. 1 Cor 15:1–11). Paul has nothing on the Sermon of the Mount, the parables or miracles recorded in the gospels! Paul exhibits a major preoccupation with suffering and its resolution in the death and Resurrection of Jesus, a focus that may be related to his earlier persecution of Christians, or the plight of human suffering he witnessed around him. Whatever the reasons, he has left us with a perverted understanding of death, alien both to the gospel of Jesus and to our contemporary efforts to reclaim a more empowering understanding of Christian Incarnation.

Some commentators seek to exonerate Paul by claiming that he meant the *meaninglessness of death* rather than death itself. Even if we had verifiable evidence that Paul actually meant that, it is not the interpretation that has been adopted either by believers in general or by Pauline scholarship for almost two thousand years. Even to our own time, a large proportion of Pauline scholars take the demonization of death at its face value.

And for Paul, there seems to be only one solution: the death and Resurrection of the historical Jesus. Death is destroyed by death, which convolutes things even further. Even a cursory glance at the gospels makes it abundantly clear that we have exaggerated and inflated the death of Jesus to a point where we have seriously neglected the liberating and empowering praxis of his life (cf. Patterson 2004, 2014). It is the life of Jesus, and not merely his death, that is salvific and redemptive. Here we encounter two serious distortions that require a quality of redress beyond my competence, and beyond the space allowed in this book. What is needed is an enlarged sense of engagement with the notion of Incarnation, in both its human and nonhuman dimensions.

Why did Jesus come on earth about two thousand years ago? To the best of my knowledge, Christian theology has not discerned a good response to this question. Since most theologians (even today) have been schooled within the context of formal religion, they tend to contextualize Jesus within that frame of reference and do so solely in terms of the Jewish religion, viewing Jesus as a fulfillment of the liberation promised in the Hebrew scriptures. But why do we confine Jesus to that context? Surely, the breakthrough wisdom of the gospels—Sermon on the Mount, Parables, Miracles—transcends formal religion in a range of significant ways.

I want to propose that we are on much more solid ground (theologically speaking) if we view Jesus in the context of our long evolutionary story of some seven million years. Assuming that our God is with us on our entire evolutionary becoming (as explored in Chapter 5), then we need to discern with a greater depth of wisdom what was transpiring during the axial period (the Christian era) of some two thousand years ago. Instead of viewing it as a strategy of *major rescue* from a fundamental flaw (original sin or whatever), should we not be discerning a different divine prerogative at work, namely, *an affirmation, confirmation, and celebration of all we humans achieved over the seven million years*, bearing in mind that we got it right for most of that time—precisely because we lived in a convivial relationship with the living earth itself.

Incarnation, therefore, does not commence with the historical Jesus, nor should it be reserved to the Christian understanding of faith. It began *seven million years ago* in East Africa. In this new evolutionary breakthrough, the divine creativity was fully at play. And it is highly unlikely that God was looking down the timeline, deciding to birth forth a new life-form, while simultaneously entertaining second thoughts that it would take some seven million years before this new life-form could be declared to be saved. That entire conceptual construal is so convoluted that it seems to me no sincere religious believer would take it seriously.

In the spirit of St. Paul's assertive declaration, we need to acknowledge that when God says YES, God means YES! (cf. 2 Cor 1:20). A God who looks over his shoulders with possible regret for what he has created sounds ominously like another projection of a confused patriarch, fearful that his power might be undermined. As a species, we need to take seriously God's unconditional affirmation of all that is created. Therefore, the Christian Jesus marks an evolutionary moment of culmination, not one of ideological rectification. Moreover, the frequent New Testament allusions to *fulfillment* (cf. Matt 5:17–18; Lk 24:27; Acts 2:36) support that same outcome, and with it, Jesus also can be seen as a bridge-builder to our next evolutionary stage, currently taking place within and around us.

Could the Resurrection of Jesus—acknowledging its several complexities—not be viewed as a promising horizon of what we humans are destined to become at further stages of our evolutionary development, endowed with supersensory abilities, including the possibility of moving between different embodied states? At the Easter vigil in Rome, April 15, 2006, Pope Benedict XVI said, "If we may borrow the language of the theory of evolution, the Resurrection is the greatest mutation, absolutely the most critical leap into a totally new dimension that there has ever been in the long history of life: a leap into a completely new order that does concern us and concerns the whole of history." This amazing insight suggests that the Resurrection of Jesus marks a new evolutionary threshold, pointing the way toward the future destiny of our human species. Without in any way denying, or challenging, some divine transformation related to Jesus himself, it declares an evolutionary breakthrough for humankind unprecedented in previous developments.

Life and death are inextricably intertwined, with death serving as the catalyst for novel evolutionary possibilities. In the historical Jesus, both dimensions interweave into that new gospel
dynamic known as the Kingdom of God (the new companionship described above). The transformation envisaged in the New
Reign of God is the end of all meaningless death, the healing of
all that has been fragmented and broken by human deviation.
And the purpose is not about reversing some primordial defor-
mity but to restore life to its authentic empowering possibilities,
captivated in the oft-cited phrase from the Gospel of John: "I
have come that they may have life and have it to the full"
(Jn 10:10).

Incarnation is about the fullness of life, an evolutionary aspiration always beckoning us from the future, in the luring awakening of the Spirit who forever energizes fresh breakthrough and
possibility. The covenant that seals our faith is not just about
a pact made with Abraham, Moses, or whoever. Rather as the
philosopher Jason Hill so well expresses it, "To make a covenant
means that one keeps looking forward, that one embraces the
greatest expression of freedom, because the covenant points
the way to the highest form of self-realization possible" (Hill
2000, x). This is an attractive aspiration indeed, and one that can
embrace and include even the darkness of pain and suffering—
the great paradox explored throughout this chapter.

Salvation: A Human Responsibility

There is nothing to be gained therefore by gazing up at a tortured martyr on the Cross and beseeching his forgiveness for
sinners or his miraculous intervention to make the world a better
place. In contemporary theological language, we are the body
of Christ on earth today. It is up to us to take over from where
Jesus left off. And that challenge is postulated on the prophetic,
subversive nature of his life, not on the bizarre torturous death
he underwent.

Jesus was not crucified as a common criminal, nor did he choose to die in order to take away the sins of the world. Jesus was killed by Roman/Jewish imperialists, and the method they used was crucifixion, a death penalty for those who rose up against the status quo, posing a threat to the powerful hegemony of those who thought they were in control. There is nothing holy, salvific, or redemptive in such a brutal death. It is the price that Jesus paid for living so radically, and the price we too may have to pay when we work subversively to rid the world of the domination and manipulation that causes so much unjust suffering and so many untimely deaths.

Nor should the Resurrection be understood as an imperial glorification of a divine hero. As indicated above, we can view it as God's ultimate vindication that Jesus's life was not given in vain. It is the confirmation of that same life as it now continues to flourish in the witnesses who continued the subversive empowering vision. Mary Magdalene and her group of followers, *and not the twelve*, are the ones who took forward that radical option for new life.

The incarnational mission of contemporary Christians is to rid the world of all meaningless suffering. That is what Jesus sought to do; and that too is what Christian codisciples should be about in every age. It is not about getting ourselves tortured or crucified in some kind of self-induced martyrdom, but rather doing everything within our power to reduce and eliminate the cruel suffering that disempowers humans and, today, leaves the earth body itself in a tortured, exploited state. So much healing and restoration awaits our incarnational response, for the sake of the new companionship of empowering discipleship.

Chapter 9

Christian Uniqueness Revisited

The idea that Christianity, or even the biblical faiths, have a monopoly on religious truth is an outrageous and absurd religious chauvinism.

—Rosemary Radford Ruether

The greatest battle, however, the battle that is waged within the soul of each person and that has been responsible for the majority of atrocities that continue to plague us today, remains unwon. The battle I am referring to, of course, is the battle against tribalism.

—Jason D. Hill

As laypeople begin to understand the Christian faith with greater wisdom and insight, they begin to question many inherited truths, often manifesting a distinctive unease with Christianity's long claim to a quality—and quantity—of truth above and beyond all other religions. Central to this claim is the uniqueness of the historical Jesus, proclaimed to be the *only one* who has authentically embodied God on earth, with the further assertion that Jesus is the only one who ever can be a true embodiment of God.

This claim tends to be based on a literalist interpretation of scripture, citing a number of well-known texts such as Acts 4:12 (No other name by which we are saved); John 10:30 (I and the Father are one); 1 Peter 3:18 (For Christ died once and for all); 1 Corinthians 3:11 (Jesus is the only foundation). Many of these texts in their original use probably served a liturgical purpose while also possibly being used to uphold belief in the one God over against the perceived threat of *false* Gods.

On closer examination, it is the imperial patriarchal will to power that creates and fosters this arrogant claim. Jesus is god's one and only Son, the only authentic revelation of the Father, the new Davidic Messiah who alone can rescue and redeem wayward humanity. Seeking to control flawed humanity, patriarchal males declared God to be a ruling king whose salvation is mediated downward through a royal line, with significant males as key collaborators, a role that bishops and clergy fulfilled in a very explicit way after the Council of Trent in the sixteenth century.

Uniqueness as a Theological Issue

The Christian claim to uniqueness has a long history, seeking to safeguard what was deemed to be an unassailable truth. In a previous work, I briefly examined the cultural and religious impact of the Jewish notion of the chosen people (O'Murchu 2015). As far back as the third century, the Christian church claimed a monopoly on truth with the declaration "Outside the Church there's no salvation." The expression originated with Cyprian of Carthage (c.200–58) and has frequently been invoked, notably by Pope Innocent III (1208), in the bull *Unam Sanctam* of Pope Boniface VIII (1302), and in the profession of faith of the Council of Florence (1442). This claim to Christian uniqueness is not merely an ecclesiastical injunction. It is an assertion by a church that had become ensnared in a debilitating cosmology (worldview), which in our time needs serious reevaluation.

It is a three-tier worldview, with heaven above, hades (the realm of the damned) below, and humans inhabiting an in-between sphere, sin-ridden and corrupt—requiring redemption by an unique divine intervention. Aided by the divine rescuer, humans are taken out of this vale of tears so that they can escape to the one and only place that can guarantee ultimate fulfillment (a process known as salvation or redemption). More precisely, it is the immortal soul and not the embodied person who will be saved. Salvation means release into the upper realm known as heaven; damnation means ending up in hell, often considered the dark and dangerous underworld.

This three-tier worldview has long lost its credibility—and outlived its usefulness—although several strands of conventional religion still cling to it. The church, and only the church, holds the key to deliverance, salvation in the hereafter. Only the guardians of the truth, the male patriarchal leaders of the church have access to the deposit of truth, inherited from the apostles. For much of Christian history, this resulted in a literal interpretation of scripture with little to no cognizance of the cultural, social, political, and religious influences that led to the formulation of the scriptures in the first place and their interpretation down through the ages.

As with modern Islam, Christians have long assumed that the revealed truth of scripture was handed down mysteriously from God to those who wrote the various books of the Bible. The words in the written text are those communicated directly by God, and such a God cannot err. The claim to the irrefutability of scripture goes something like this: Jesus was the Son of God (quite literally), God's one and only incarnate presence on earth. Particularly through the power of his death and Resurrection, Jesus brought about a divine rescue for which there is no parallel in any other religion. And what Jesus declared to be the truth was passed on by the twelve apostles, recorded by the inspired writers of scripture (particularly St. Paul and the four evangelists), inscribed in the books of the Bible (especially in the

New Testament) and entrusted to the male patriarchal church for authentic interpretation.

The early Christian protagonists were at heart fiercely monotheistic Jews who viewed Jesus as uniquely endowed with a divine identity. The Shema (Dt 6:4) declares that there is one Lord (Yahweh), and Paul affirms that the one Lord is Jesus Christ who is creator of all and the source of our existence (1 Cor 8:6). And for the early Jewish-Christians, King David was the prototype for the messianic deliverance that it was believed Jesus would fulfill. Thus, we witness a patriarchal line of descent (as in Matt 1:1–17 and Lk 3: 23–38) in which the historical Jesus becomes wrapped up in a cult of domination, already in his time enculturated in the divine right of kings and their prerogative for violent liberation.

How the average Christian viewed the process—for the first three centuries—is now impossible to retrieve, except for occasional glimpses provided by archaeologists and ancient historians. What is beyond dispute is the tragic triumphalism of Roman Emperor Constantine early in the fourth century. Christianity's climb to dominance begins with the conversion of Emperor Constantine (d.337CE). Constantine was involved in a bitter civil war to retain the emperor's throne. Before the decisive clash with Maxentius, his brother-in-law and chief rival in 312, it is claimed that he experienced a vision where Christ appeared to him, instructing him to place the sign of Christ on the banners carried by his troops. He did so, and his army proceeded to demolish the rival opposition. He credited the Christian God for his resounding victory and proceeded to favor Christianity over all other religions throughout his massive empire.

Almost overnight, Christianity was propelled to the status of a global, theological powerhouse. In the words of Wendy Farley (2011, 189), "When Constantine gained his military victory under the sign of the Cross, the conflation of the Kingdom of God and the Empire of Caesar became an essential part of Christian history and theology." In the space of just one century—the fourth of the Christian era—fourteen church councils were convened, nearly all at the behest of the emperor. Roman citizens and subjects converted in droves, as Christians were afforded special tax breaks and other amenities not available to members of any other religious affiliation.

All other religions were outlawed by Constantine. It would not be until later in the fourth century (380 CE), that Christianity was declared to be the official state religion of Rome, making illegal all other models of worship. This would ensure the conversion of nearly everyone under Roman control, covering much of Europe, West Asia, and North Africa. Failing to convert could result in deportation or execution.

Constantine favored Christianity for one main reason: it could/would be a powerful force for unity throughout the empire. His goal was inclusivity but envisaged for reasons far from noble and very much at variance with the Jesus he proclaimed to be *Pantocrator* (Ruler of the Universe). Constantine's religious aspiration was *conformity, control, and domination.* The Christian religion was the tool that would reinforce his unilateral power, a very different aspiration from the gospel's Companionship of Empowerment, described in Chapter 6.

Challenging the Monopoly

Indeed it was not until the mid-twentieth century that this patriarchal monopoly was seriously challenged for the first time. In September 1943, Pope Pius XII issued an encyclical letter, *Divino Afflante Spiritu* (Inspired by the Holy Spirit) calling for new translations of the Bible from the original languages (apart from Latin), while also encouraging textual criticism and the use of the historical–critical method, thus launching a new critical approach to the study of scripture. The Catholic scholar Raymond E. Brown described it as a Magna Carta for biblical progress.

Both scripture scholars and theologians embarked upon a new dialogue with the world and the culture of the time, moving rather quickly to reestablish the primacy of God's New Reign on earth, a radical novel way for empowering companionship. The Catholic Council known as Vatican II sought to further extend this *renewal*, but as is widely known, it has been a haphazard process with huge ambivalence, particularly from within the Catholic hierarchy itself.

Meanwhile it was the Catholic laity, progeny of the culture of mass information, aroused into a new curiosity, and inspired by an expanding spiritual hunger, that created a new threshold for faith in the twenty-first century, with substantial implications for our expanded understanding of Incarnation. It is to that clientele that the Irish scholar John Feehan (2012, 148) addresses these words:

> When you are confronted by evidence that the faith in which you were brought up no longer provides an adequate explanation for the nature, meaning and purpose of your life, you have three choices. You can refuse to accept the evidence and continue as before. You can abandon the faith you grew up with because it has proved to be inadequate. Or, third, *you can accept the new knowledge and use it to develop a more mature understanding of what lies at the core of your beliefs.* The first response is spiritually dishonest. The second is spiritual laziness. *The third is a stance of critical acceptance, leading to a reinterpretation of core concepts. . . . It requires courage and a plethora of other virtues that have been gathering dust in your spirit.* Every advance in understanding invites us into a deeper faith. (Emphasis mine.)

For this new reflective and critical generation, the traditional claims to Christian uniqueness are often viewed as arrogant, imperialistic, and ideological. It is felt to be more a betrayal of the new companionship than, in any way, an authentic assertion of an incarnational faith. And as is evidenced in other world religions, it readily leads to a kind of colonial domination, frequently accompanied by violent persecution of the other, perceived to be a God-less threat.

Claims for the uniqueness of Christ, and the universal redemption that only Christianity can deliver, still reverberate from the formal ecclesiastical enclaves, but that is not where many reflective Christians are to be found anymore. Indeed, the more the spiritual awakening gains popularity, the more reactionary the preachers and teachers tend to become. And all this is transpiring into a daily interactive culture where millions rub shoulders with others of different cultures, ethnicity, and faith, where most are not particularly worried what religious camp one belongs to, and where they will happily engage in a deeper conversation, as long as it promotes fresh hope, peace, and human empowerment.

We must also acknowledge that in the evolving cultures of the twenty-first century, *multiple belonging* is extensively embraced (cf. Goosen 2011).While national identities still dictate legal and political transactions, economic and cultural undertakings operate out of a more globalized agenda, where megacorporations and not nation-states command the upper hand. In this complex globalized milieu, religions fare poorly, having lost nearly all semblance of moral imperative, and are often viewed as anachronistic and irrelevant to the pressing cultural issues of our age.

And filling the vacuum is a vast range of spiritual endeavors, with a complex mixture of mystics, gurus, charlatans, and demagogues. Despite this crazy mix, few can deny that something profound and prophetic is at work in this emerging awakening often described as modern spirituality (cf. Johnson and Ord 2012 for a fine overview). It clearly appeals to the millions of disillusioned religionists and provides yet another dent in the armor of the one-time religious monopoly.

In a word, the incarnational body of contemporary Christianity engages the modern world with a fluidity and versatility that formal religion can neither comprehend nor wrestle with. It sometimes feels like formal religion might have lost the plot—due to what is inscribed in the heart of the profession of the Christian faith—acknowledging the man Jesus as the *Only Son*, the *only mediator between God and humankind*, and the *only Savior*! Despite this postmodern fluidity, or perhaps, because of it, Christian scholars involved in multifaith dialogue—in the closing decades of the twentieth century—raised fresh concerns about the uniqueness of Jesus, fearing that it might be compromised and diluted amid the widening landscape of religious tolerance and the mutual acceptance of differing views.

Beyond Interreligious Dialogue

As we move deeper into the twenty-first century, interreligious dialogue continues to engage a range of scholars and spiritual seekers on a global scale. Paul Copan (2007) provides a valuable theological overview. The Parliament of the World's Religions has enjoyed a significant revival.[1] Interfaith work expanded exponentially around the globe in the 1990s and into the twenty-first century, with the formation of interfaith, multicultural efforts like the Pluralism Project (Harvard University 1991), Interfaith Center at the Presidio (1995), Chicago-based Interfaith Worker Justice (1996), the Interfaith Center of New York (1997), the United Religions Initiative (2000), World Council of Religious Leaders (2002), Interfaith Youth Core (2002), the Charter for

---

[1] In 1988 nearly one hundred years had passed since the World's Congress of Religions and Vivekananda's historic speech. A group of religious leaders and local organizers in Chicago came together to plan a centennial celebration, and through this, the Council for a Parliament of the World's Religions came into being. In 1993, the parliament hosted its conference in Chicago with eight thousand participants from faith backgrounds around the world. The organization went on to host meetings around the world every few years: Cape Town in 1999; Barcelona in 2004; Melbourne in 2009; Brussels in 2014; and the first US conference since 1993, took place in Salt Lake City in 2015.

Compassion (2009), and President Obama's Interfaith and Community Service Campus Challenge (2010).

Multifaith dialogue in the 1990s was largely a Christian endeavor, with minimal participation from other religious adherents (notably Muslims and evangelical Christians).[2]

As a scholarly enterprise, multifaith dialogue has lost much of its original momentum, getting stuck in the theological preoccupation about the uniqueness of Jesus (which really means the superiority of the Christian Christ). However, the dialogue has continued unabated, assuming a range of cultural articulations, as increasing numbers of people in our multicultural world rub shoulders on a daily basis with other creeds and religious affiliations. Not merely do we study each other's faith systems, but we engage in shared spiritual practices such as meditation and contemplative prayer, and join together in special festivals such as the Hindu *Dwalai,* and the Muslim *Eid.* Among adult Christians, many quite comfortably share ecumenical sacramental practices, especially in communal celebrations such as marriages and funerals.

The twenty-first century marks a significant advance in religious tolerance, despite the fact that intolerance has become

---

[2] Some of the key Christian names included Hans Kung, Harvey Cox, John Hick, Paul F. Knitter, John D'Arcy May, Raimon Panikkar, M.Thomas Thangaraj, David Tracy, and Felix Wilfred. On October 13, 2007, Muslims expanded their message; in *A Common Word between Us and You,* 138 Muslim scholars, clerics, and intellectuals unanimously came together for the first time since the days of the Prophet to declare the common ground between Christianity and Islam. From January 6–11, 2009, at Gujarat's Mahuva, the Dalai Lama inaugurated an interfaith "World Religions-Dialogue and Symphony" conference convened by Hindu preacher Morari Bapu. This conference explored ways and means to deal with the discord among major religions; participants included Professor Samdhong Rinpoche on Buddhism, Diwan Saiyad Zainul Abedin Ali Sahib (Ajmer Sharif) on Islam, Dr. Prabalkant Dutt on non-Catholic Christianity, Swami Jayendra Saraswathi on Hinduism, and Dastur Dr. Peshtan Hormazadiar Mirza on Zoroastrianism. Gerard Mannion (2015) provides a valuable overview on multifaith dialogue at the present time.

conspicuous and favored by public media. Such intolerance seems to be noticeably more overt among Middle Eastern and North African Muslims (with ISIL being exceptionally violent), but there have also been some vicious examples from Buddhism in both Sri Lanka and Myanmar, among Hindus in parts of India, and pockets of extreme Christian fundamentalism in the United States and elsewhere.

In the present chapter, I want to trace the growing popularity of religious tolerance and pluralism among Christians, and its contribution to a Christian embodied presence, which I will claim is more liberating, empowering, enriching, and theologically more generic for incarnational growth and advancement. While many critics fear a slide into postmodern fluidity, relativism, syncretism, and compromise of truth, I am trying to reclaim biblical and theological foundations for prioritizing our commonalities rather than emphasizing our differences. As a religion postulated first and foremost on a God of love, what binds us together as Christians is far more significant than what separates us into denominational enclaves.

Uniqueness and Revelation

To facilitate this new breakthrough, we need to revisit—and redefine—some key theological concepts. To the fore is the notion of *revelation*, which we have already encountered in Chapter 2. The word *revelation* suggests the disclosure or clarification of something or someone previously hidden or unavailable to human comprehension. It's like opening a curtain or a door and seeing what is behind it. The Christian notion of revelation, then, is the act of revealing or disclosing something that has not been known or seen before, and in strict Christian terms, only came to the fore fully in the life, death, and Resurrection of Jesus.

Contemporary adult faith seekers feel distinctly uncomfortable around this claim. It smacks of Christian imperialism, a kind of anthropocentric arrogance characteristic of classical Greek metaphysics. It seems to dismiss or at least undermine the divine creativity that flourished throughout our human incarnational story of seven million years. And worse still, it fails to see the creative empowerment of the Great Spirit at work in the whole creation for billions of years. For contemporary faith seekers, it is not so much a theological claim as an outrageous ideological reductionism.

For the embodied, incarnational faith of the twenty-first century, we need to respect and cooperate with the divine initiative manifested throughout the eons of evolution. In a word, let's begin where God begins in time. God's first and enduring revelation, the divine outpouring, happens in the cosmic creation, understood as universe or multiverse. That is the *primary* revelation that deepens and complexifies long before the human species, religions, or churches ever evolved, similar to what Karl Rahner one time called *universal-transcendental revelation.*[3]

---

[3] Among Catholic theologians, the late Karl Rahner seems to have adopted an understanding of revelation quite congenial to the expansive view I outline in this book. Rahner distinguishes two kinds of revelation: universal-transcendental revelation and special-categorical revelation. While the first refers to the experience of God that could happen anywhere and for everyone, the latter is an expression of the former within the special revelation of Jesus Christ. When it comes to the human, Rahner is even better known for his controversial category of the anonymous Christian. Every human being is graced with an openness to ultimate mystery, which mystery is made real and tangible for all people in the historical Jesus. For Rahner, *grace* and *presence* are interchangeable, a self-communication of the God who is ever intimately present to all persons, precisely because this same God inhabits the whole creation. This strikes me, as having affinities with the notion of the Great Spirit outlined in Chapter 3.

With regard to the notion of revelation, Rahner (1978, 78–203) maintains that the universal history of salvation is also the history of revelation. God's presence as grace is the central, factual revelation of Judeo-Christian salvation history. Revelation is presence flowing through the mental realms of the human personality. Presence pervades the conscious, semiconscious, and unconscious horizons of every person. These issues are explored at length in Rahner's *Spirit in the World* (1968) and *Grace in Freedom* (1969),

Our human appropriation of that revelation happens first and foremost in and through the created order of which we are an integral part, and as I suggest in Chapter 3, the spirituality of the Great Spirit may well be our most reliable path to appropriating this expansive understanding of revelation.

Unfortunately, for many contemporary theologians, uniqueness denotes superiority and exclusion. Our Christian-based faith is deemed to be superior to all others—only the Christian Jesus embodies the totality of truth—and consequently, all other religions are inferior to varying degrees. For the twenty-first century, and for adult faith seekers of our time, those claims are too congealed, representing the restrictive context of formal religion. Furthermore, the focus is too anthropocentric, failing to honor the timeless revelation of the Holy One not merely in humans, but in every aspect of the cosmic and planetary creation.

For incarnational faith for the twenty-first century, God's prodigious revelation is in the whole creation, and therein lies its true uniqueness. It opens up enlarged horizons for living out our faith in the name of love and justice. Therefore, even the destructive elements of creation—described above as the Great Paradox—must be seen as integral to God's revelation. Engaging such a revelatory paradoxical universe requires a quality of theologically informed discernment, not extensively evidenced in the modern world.

Uniqueness and Singular Religious Allegiance

John Hick (d.2012), perhaps the most notable religious pluralist today, calls for a Copernican revolution of religions. Cosmology has shifted from a Ptolemaic geocentric (earth-centered) view of the universe to a Copernican heliocentric (sun-centered) one. Similarly, we must replace a Christocentric view, claiming Chris-

---

while his main outline on revelation is available in *Foundations of Christian Faith* (1978).

tianity to be the only true religion, with a God/reality-centered view, in which all religions, including Christianity, offer partial apertures into the mystery of reality, but none has an exclusive monopoly over it.

This position encounters outright rejection by the teaching authority of the Catholic Church and by other Christians of a more fundamentalist persuasion. The accusation of *relativism* is made loud and strong, which basically declares that *absolutism*, as understood by these sources, is the only way to access the fullness of truth. But *whose absolutes,* we need to ask, by what criteria are such absolutes considered to be authentic? In this regard, adult faith seekers of the twenty-first century are quick to point out that our inherited doctrine of revelation and the accompanying notion of biblical inspiration are notions drawn up in the third and fourth Christian centuries by a small, elite group of Caucasian males, many heavily influenced by Constantine's passion for domination, control, and conformity. Ninety percent of God's people at that time had no say whatsoever; females were totally excluded, and the other creatures sharing with us the web of life had no say either. Surely, any God who is that narrowly selective cannot hope to command either the credibility or allegiance of adult faith seekers in our time, immersed as we are in the generic evolutionary thrust of this age, which seeks to honor complexity and diversity?

John Hick does not naively insist that *all religions are basically the same.* For Hick (1995), religious belief is the result of culturally conditioned attempts to arrive at the Ultimate Reality. There are different ways of conceiving, experiencing, and responding to this Ultimate Reality. And none of them can be declared to be absolute, because to do so plunges us straight into idolatry, playing God, and ignoring our relative human wisdom, which at all times can only comprehend reality in a partial and limited way.

What then of role of official teaching authority? Perhaps, there is a better question: why a distinctive teaching authority in the first place? And of course the answer is because humans are perceived to be a sinful species, largely deluded and incapable of comprehending deep truth. This is not what we detect in our long evolutionary story when humans seem to have gotten it right most of the time. It looks like the flawed anthropology might be that of the very people who claim to have a monopoly of ultimate truth!

Unique Truth or Unique Power

This brings us to what might be the most tantalizing and formidable issue of all: *the human investment in patriarchal power.* This, I suggest, is what the claim to uniqueness is really about. It has nothing to do with God (other than the God of our patriarchal projections), nor with revealed truth. It is the critical issue frequently named throughout this book—probably to the point of tedium for some readers. It is the new human orientation adopted by leading males in the wake of the Agricultural Revolution, when a select group of aggressive, violent males set out to conquer and control all before them, relegating the living earth itself to a commodity for human usufruct, assigning males as managerial procreators, and consigning females to the curse of the ground upon which they stand (cf. Gn 3:17).

The power is vested in the controlling male who then goes on to consolidate that power by projecting it onto the imperial divinity who resides above and outside the sin-laden earth. With this deviant development, humans abandoned their allegiance to the Great Spirit and, more controversially, rapidly lost faith in the Great Goddess, the embodied feminine divinity who seems to have been the primary guide for much of the Paleolithic era. Now, only one God can be tolerated, obeyed, and worshipped, the one that will entitle the patriarchs themselves to exercise unquestioned and unique power.

This new powerful God mediates domination through one earthly representative: the male king! Therefore, the divine liberator would have to descend from a royal line (cf. Matt 1.1–17; Lk

3:23–38), and ironically the ideal model invoked at the time was King David, deemed by contemporary researchers to have been a brutal dictator who abused and eliminated even his own relatives to procure his absolute control. And Jesus was expected to follow in his footsteps, and some still expect Jesus to fulfill that role! Power dies slowly.

Despite the fact that Jesus seems to have totally disowned this craze for power, and instead invested in an empowering counterculture named in this book as the *Companionship of Empowerment,* the prophetic dream became dislodged amid the imperial onslaught of Constantine and all who colluded with him. And those who did collude reaped rich gains, including several church leaders of the time. Thus, Christianity embarked upon a long misplaced journey where the power of truth succumbed to the truth of power. Christian uniqueness became fixated with the protection and promotion of such power. So potent was the monopoly that even the Protestant Reformation did little to undermine its resilience. It began to crumble in the late nineteenth century and is likely to collapse substantially in the next few decades.

While adult faith seekers identify the fixation on uniqueness as a religious preoccupation with power, most churches, and their respective authorities, have not yet faced the embarrassing truth. It has all the resemblance of the proverbial adage *old soldiers don't die, they simply fade away.* The power implodes on itself, sometimes amid renewed waves of violence (possibly what is happening through the Islamic ISIL in the second decade of the twenty-first century); rancor and disintegration sets in; the remnant clings on desperately, while all the while, the Spirit weaves a new loom, till, eventually, in a classical paschal journey, Calvary gives way to Resurrection.

Power can conquer many things, but in the end, another uniqueness endures, the empowering liberation, incarnated in the Christian notion of the New Reign of God. As I indicate in previous works (O'Murchu 2011, 2014a), I do believe that there is a uniqueness to our Christian faith that we can justifiably be proud of, described in earlier chapters as the *Companionship of Empowerment*. It provides a blistering critique of all power seeking, conjuring an alternative option for power sharing, and the empowerment of all have been disenfranchised by manipulation and exploitation—see the fine exposition in the works of American scripture scholar Wes Howard-Brook (2010, 2016). And included in that vision is the living earth itself along with all the other creatures with whom we share the web of life. In this expanded context, uniqueness is obtained not by stressing differences, but in the celebration and affirmation of commonalities.

Chapter 10

Advent and Christmas:
Incarnational Reinterpretation

We know grace first through our bodies.

—Tertullian

The birth stories subvert the dominant consciousness of the first century world as well as our own. Jesus' followers learned well how to tell subversive stories ... We who have seen the star and heard the angels sing are called to participate in the new birth and in the new world proclaimed by these stories.

—Marcus Borg and John Dominic Crossan

In our Christian faith story, Incarnation is associated primarily with Christmas and the arrival of Jesus in our midst as a divine–human being, happening for the first time about two thousand years ago. And for the Christian church, from early times, this was a ritualized feast, not merely marked by a special celebration, but also anticipated in a manner requiring a distinctive quality of preparation. Just as Lent signified a time of preparation for the

189

celebration of Easter, so Advent was the ecclesiastical season to ready ourselves for the event that commemorates and celebrates God's unique coming to our earth.

Initially, there was little connection between Advent and Christmas. At least in fourth- and fifth-century Spain and Gaul, Advent was a season of preparation for the baptism of new Christians that would take place on January 6, feast of the Epiphany. Three gospel features in the life of Jesus are brought together in this celebration: the visit of the Magi to the baby Jesus (Matt 2:1), his baptism in the Jordan River by John the Baptist (Jn 1:29), and the first miracle at Cana (Jn 2:1). Christians would spend forty days in penance, prayer, and fasting to prepare for this special occasion.[1]

By the sixth century, however, Roman Christians had tied Advent to *the coming of Christ*, not Christ's first coming in the manger of Bethlehem, but his second coming in judgment at the end of time. It was not until the Middle Ages that the Advent season was explicitly linked to Christ's first coming at Christmas.

According to the *New Catholic Encyclopedia*, Advent today is meant to serve the following purposes:

---

[1] The ninth canon of the first Council of Macon, held in 582, ordained that during the same interval between St. Martin's day and Christmas, the Mondays, Wednesdays, and Fridays, should be fasting days, and that the sacrifice should be celebrated according to the Lenten rite. Not many years before that, namely in 567, the second Council of Tours had enjoined the monks to fast from the beginning of December till Christmas. This practice of penance soon extended to the whole forty days, even for the laity: and it was commonly called St. Martin's Lent. The capitularia of Charlemagne, in the sixth book, leave us in no doubt on the matter; and Rabanus Maurus, in the second book of his Institution of clerics, bears testimony to this observance. There were even special rejoicings made on St. Martin's feast, just as we see them practiced now at the approach of Lent and Easter. The first allusion to Advent being reduced to four weeks is to be found in the ninth century, in a letter of Pope St. Nicholas I to the Bulgarians. The Greek church still continues to observe the fast of Advent, though with much less rigor than that of Lent.

- The faithful should prepare themselves worthily to celebrate the anniversary of the Lord's coming into the world as the incarnate God of love.
- In this way, the faithful will make their souls fitting abodes for the Redeemer coming in Holy Communion and through grace.
- Finally, so that the faithful can make themselves ready for His final coming as judge, at death, and at the end of the world.

There is, therefore, a first coming, and a final coming, with the people of God meant to be in a perpetual state of waiting for God to intervene. This suggests that we humans never stand a chance of getting it right. We are always waiting for further divine intervention, a kind of religious codependency that keeps us passive, insecure, ambivalent and childlike. This sounds like patriarchal religiosity rather than anything to do with God or Christian Incarnation.

Worth recalling at this stage, is the oft-quoted phrase of scripture scholar John Dominic Crossan (2010, 89–90): *We are waiting for God's intervention, but God is waiting for our collaboration.* The God who calls us forth as codisciples, as friends and not servants (cf. Jn 15:15), seems to represent a different divine initiative from what is portrayed above. And the God who has befriended our species through our long evolutionary story, with the grace of mutual empowerment, does not seem to be a divine figurehead overly concerned with safeguarding divine power against the wiles of sinful humans. Nor, it seems, have our First Nations brothers and sisters ever been too enamored about this harsh judgmental figure reigning above the clouds, waiting to strike hard at the end of time, because they have never known God as a celestial imperial ruler; that portrayal of God, as indicated in previous chapters of this book, is a much more recent invention.

Collaboration with the Divine

We come to the Christmas season, focused on the infancy narratives of Matthew and Luke. Worthy of note is the understanding adopted by Marcus Borg and John Dominic Crossan (2007) in their popular outline of the Christmas story. Far from the conventional devotional emphasis, embellished amid the secular and religious consumerism of our time, we are confronted with a biblical narrative in which the Roman imperialism of the day is consistently undermined, particularly in the rich symbolism adopted by the evangelists in the infancy narratives. The *Pax Romana* of Caesar Augustus is outwitted by Jesus the prince of peace; Jesus robs from Caesar Augustus his original claim to the title, Savior of the World; for Matthew, the wise Magi come from the East, not from the Roman West; for Luke, the shepherds hail the new born king subverting the kingship of the great King David, one time a shepherd himself (1 Sm 16:11, 17:15).

> The stories of the first Christmas are both personal and political. They speak of personal and political transformation. Set in their first century context, they are comprehensive and passionate visions of another way of seeing life and of living our lives. . . . The stories of the first Christmas are pervasively anti-imperial. (Borg and Crossan, 2007, viii–ix)

Accordingly, the Christmas narrative invites us not to a devotional admiration for the imperial child of a distant reigning God, but to an adult countercultural solidarity with all who are oppressed and kept outside by imperial exclusion. We need, therefore, to reimagine, the chief characters, particularly Mary and Joseph, not simply as obedient servants to a miraculous irruption of daily life, but rather as prophetic collaborators in launching the New Reign of God (the new companionship), which was to be the major thrust of Jesus's entire existence as both child and adult.

We can never hope to reconstruct what historical significance Matthew and Luke attribute to Joseph, if indeed any. The symbolic and metaphorical significance is what we need to discern. For Matthew, Joseph holds a central place in the dynastic line of descent from King David (not so for Luke, where the descent is through Mary, rather than Joseph). And Matthew, who seems to have written his gospel for a Jewish audience, makes several explicit links with the Hebrew scriptures. In the case of Joseph, scholars have noted the following parallels between Jacob's son Joseph (in Genesis) and the New Testament Joseph:

- *Both have fathers named Jacob* (Matt 1:16; Gn 30:22–24), Heli in the case of Luke's genealogy (cf. Lk 3:23).
- *Both received dreams from God* (Matt 1:20–21; Gn 37:5–11).
- *Both were righteous and chaste* (Matt. 1:19; Gn 39:7–18).
- *Both saved their families by taking them to Egypt* (Matt 2:13; Gn 45:16–20).

These parallels are usually interpreted as confirmation of Jesus's messianic identity. The deliverer foreseen in the first Joseph comes to full flowering in the second, thus bringing to fulfillment all that God had promised of old. In terms of Incarnation, this interpretation fits the conventional understanding of Jesus serving a divine intervention to rescue sinful humanity. It is not the understanding I am adopting throughout the present study.

So, does Joseph have anything to offer for the expanded understanding of Incarnation I am exploring? According to Jewish mythology, one of the messianic expectations was the reunification of the people of Israel as one nation. According to Genesis 29, the patriarch Jacob had two sons, Judah and Joseph. The descendants of Judah became the dominant tribe in the south, and those of Joseph dominated the north, and for long a fierce rivalry prevailed between the two. While Matthew traces Jesus's credentials through the Judean line, he culminates it with Joseph.

Symbolically, we can see that in Jesus the two Jewish patriarchs are united as one. The historical Jesus serves as the archetypal force seeking to unite all that divides and heal all that fragments.

One also wonders if the emphasis on Joseph as an older person had any traditional significance for the Jewish context. It certainly resonates with our contemporary sensibilities around the emergence of wise elders (see Chapter 1). Joseph, the great dreamer, also exhibits remarkable wisdom, attuned to the unfolding mystery of divine–human birthing, but he is also remarkably adept at the practicalities of domestic duty and protective care. We also see the wise elder unfolds in the Lukan narrative of temple purification: Simeon (Lk 2:25ff.) and the prophetess Anna (Lk 2:36ff.).

We now turn our attention to Mary who has been traditionally depicted as the great collaborator with the divine imperative, but it is a quality of collaboration alien to our modern understanding of incarnational mutuality. In Christian art Mary tends to be depicted as a young Caucasian, looking very devotional, obedient, and subservient. Catholics claim that she was herself immaculately conceived at birth and elevated straight from earth to heaven at her death. Her body seems to be an obstacle that has to be rendered redundant as far as possible, in case there might be any residue of human sin or frailty that would make her unsuitable as a carrier of divine life.

Her pregnancy and birth of Jesus is shrouded in mystery, allegedly impregnated not by any human male but by some unique intervention of the Holy Spirit of God. From the perspective of the Great Spirit (see Chapter 3), this claim makes a great deal of sense, as the Spirit is the primary energizer of all creative endeavors, including human fertilization—the difference being that human agency is largely subverted in the case of Mary.

Mary is declared to be a *virgin*, which in biological terms means that her hymen has not been penetrated and therefore she has never had sexual intercourse with a man. However, as many commentators point out, in describing Mary's virginity, we encounter a confusing picture between the Greek *parthenos* and the Hebrew *almah* (cf. Is 7:14). The latter has nothing to do with biological virginity (*bethulah* being the pertinent word). Rather it denotes a young woman of marriageable age and of outstanding character. Theologian Elizabeth Johnson (2003, 239) affirms a more ancient and archetypal meaning for virginity: "To be a virgin is to be one in yourself, free, independent, insubordinated, unexploited, a woman never subdued."

What we are dealing with here is an idealization, heavily contaminated with what Elizabeth Johnson (2003, 28) describes as "an increasingly strong torrent of misogyny against women and their bodies." The ramifications for women over many centuries have been devastating, but from an incarnational perspective, it has also undermined human integrity and dignity for women and men alike.

Understood in her original historical and Jewish context, Mary is not merely an impressive model of empowering Incarnation, she is actually an enduring archetype of what Incarnation can mean in its fuller scope as outlined in the present work. In this claim I am largely following the seminal and inspiring work of Elizabeth Johnson, *Truly Our Sister* (2003). I am also sympathetic to the highly controversial claim that Jesus might have been an illegitimate child, possibly the outcome of a rape by a Roman soldier (cf. Schaberg 1987). To most Christians, this is a shocking—and disgusting—suggestion!

So, why invoke it? Because it serves as a profound example of how Incarnation embraces paradox, pain, contradiction, the Jungian shadow, the many raw experiences of daily life that we prefer to disown or repress. Nothing is too gross or disgusting for incarnational engagement. If Mary was the victim of rape—a possibility suggested by Matthew's inclusion of three sexually problematic women in his genealogy, and a popular legend that even names the soldier as Panthera—then she represents the millions of women oppressed and marginalized over many centuries.

And she carries a significant potential also for the many men abused and disempowered by the patriarchal system.

But the real empowering potential of Mary does not come merely from this controversial and disputed claim, but rather from the emerging portrayal of her cultural identity and status as a Jewish woman of her day. Contrary to the subdued passivity of centuries and her pseudospiritual idealization, the historical Mary would have been a robust, industrious, multiskilled woman. In many ways, it is she who would have held home and family together. Within the family, she would have served as homemaker, weaver, educator, medicine person, and horticulturalist. Like the great goddess of ancient times, she was deeply grounded in creation, cocreating with the Great Spirit, many centuries ahead of our contemporary pneumatological wisdom.

Yes, Mary certainly collaborated with the divine, but not in the subdued, overspiritualized caricature of popular religiosity. She may well have enjoyed a collaborative relationship with an older male, named as Joseph in the gospels. And whatever her pregnant status, disreputable or otherwise, Joseph would have ensured a quality of care and hospitality not recorded in the gospels. British journalist Nick Page (2012) claims that in the cultural context of the time, Joseph's family home would have been the first option for Mary to give birth. It may have been a crowded household with a little room in the *kataluma* (meaning: inn or guest room). So they laid the baby elsewhere in the house, perhaps in a manger or animal feeding trough. The homes at the time often consisted of a two-floor division, humans sleeping upstairs and animals occupying the ground floor during the night.

According to Nick Page (2012, 24), "The story of Jesus's birth, therefore, is not one of exclusion, but inclusion. . . . Joseph's relatives made a place for Jesus in the heart of their household. They did not shun Mary, even though her status would have been suspect and even shameful (carrying an illegitimate child): they brought her inside. They made room for Jesus in the heart of a peasant's home."

Among the first guests that came through the door were shepherds, commonly regarded as social and religious outcasts, ritually suspect and socially disreputable. According to the Mishna, it was forbidden for orthodox Jews to buy wool, milk, or kids directly from herdsmen. Many of them were homeless and deprived of basic human rights. Yet, here they are as the first to welcome the one who in time would declare himself to be the Good Shepherd, with a claim to empowerment far beyond the ancient shepherd figure of King David.

And the royal kings who we use to decorate the Christmas crib give another interesting dimension to our expanded notion of Incarnation. *They were not kings at all*; Matthew describes them as wise men (cf. Matt 2:1), popularly believed to have been astrologers and possibly soothsayers. They outwit the devious King Herod, representing a wit and wisdom that the empire can neither contain nor subvert. Those that read the stars and reached for the heavens can be seen as representing something of that cosmic and planetary dimension of Incarnation explored in earlier chapters of this book.

Celebrating Emmanuel

For the Christian churches, Easter is the leading feast, when Jesus is delivered from earthly bondage to the exalted glory of being our Lord and Savior. There is no shortage of royal, patriarchal attribution in this claim, as in exalted Christian acclamations such as *Christus vincit! Christus regnat! Christus imperat (trans:* Christ conquers, Christ reigns, Christ commands). And, of course, this imperial spirituality is still widely adopted by the disenfranchised masses for whom the atoning death of Jesus has such an immediate appeal—the devotion of consolation, I describe elsewhere (O'Murchu 2014a). It falls well short, however, of the incarnational empowerment explored in the present work.

The Emmanuel of the Infancy Narratives (cf. Matt 1:23) should not be viewed in exclusive anthropocentric terms, and it certainly should not be reduced to an infantile fascination with a vulnerable baby lying in a manger. Human vulnerability is certainly at stake, but the empowerment through and beyond such fragility is the critical point. Some of the salient points need to be reclaimed and asserted afresh:

- *The Adult Jesus.* We know virtually nothing about Jesus before the age of thirty, when according to popular belief, he embarked upon his public ministry. Providing a story for his birth and childhood certainly enriches the biography, but we must acknowledge its legendary nature, and the likelihood that much of it is based on the heroic births of other famous ancient personalities. So, it is an inflated infancy, with a likely underlying patriarchal agenda that seeks to keep Christians as childlike as possible: subdued, obedient, loyal, uncritical, passive, and fearful of official authority. These are *not* dispositions of gospel discipleship, and in all probability, the historical Jesus would totally denounce the manner in which they have been used throughout Christian history. For responsible Christian faith in the twenty-first century, we must always start with the adult Jesus and the gospel project of the New Reign of God, described as the *Companionship of Empowerment* throughout the present work.

- The Great Spirit would seem to be the central character, the *persona dramatis* supreme, in the infancy narratives. That divine life force that energizes everything in creation, even before the Big Bang ever took place, is also the source of new life in this archetypal story. And the Mary who collaborated with the Great Spirit represents humanity in its enduring profundity. In many ancient cultures, the Virgin is the archetypal one who gives birth to stars and galaxies, planets and organisms, bacteria and organic creatures, angels and humans. She is indeed the handmaid of the Great Spirit, the primordial cobirther, endowed with cosmic, planetary, and human elegance.

- Birthing is God's primary activity—radiant in every aspect of creation, including its paradoxical features of birth–death–rebirth. Here the primordial creative source is not that of an outstanding patriarchal male (theologically named as God the Father), but a mother-like figure of prodigious creativity, which the historical Mary represents. Intriguingly, it is precisely when we recapture the uniqueness of Mary as a historical cultural personage (as Elizabeth Johnson [2003] does with remarkable ingenuity), that her archetypal significance is truly illuminated. In and through Mary, the womb of God and the womb of the universe are one, and birthing is the enduring legacy within which every creature—and not merely humans—is missioned for the work of cocreation.

- The Great Paradox of birth–death–rebirth is also at work in this foundational faith experience. If Jesus, as Emmanuel, was indeed an illegitimate child, and even more so, if he is the product of an act of rape, then he embodies all the vulnerabilities and travesties that belong to creation's own great paradox. To this extent, we evidence an archetypal truth in Christianity's long artistic history wherein the nativity scene tends to be depicted with risk, danger, unpredictability. In this context too, is the paradox of the Cross, not an emblem of God's sacrifice for us sinners, but a prophetic horizon shared by all who sacrifice their lives for the sake of empowering justice, the price we may have to pay to make Incarnation real on earth?

- The human face of God made manifest in the Emmanuel figure is not the dominant patriarchal male of classical Greek philosophy, but rather the relational event, representing a interdependent creative matrix. In archetypal terms, this is where the shepherds and astrologers become an integral dimension of the crib scene. From the mountain pastures to the starry skies, the angelic echoes proclaim an interdependent universe to which the human intimately belongs. Humans have known all this for a few million years before the arrival of Jesus, and in the revelatory moment of the first Christmas, all that humans have achieved is being affirmed, confirmed, and celebrated anew.

Christmas is the great Christian feast—in fact, the greatest of them all. Salvation and redemption belong first and foremost to the primordial birthing forth, not to the mighty act of dying. Resurrection has more in common with Bethlehem than with Calvary. It is indeed the renewed birth, this time facilitated through another archetypal female, namely, Mary Magdalene. Here the incarnational logic of the Christian faith comes full circle. From the cave of the original birth, another archetypal cave (the empty tomb) releases the new wave of incarnational empowerment, and the Risen One becomes the symbolic catalyst, carrying creation forward to its next evolutionary breakthrough.

Waiting for the Coming . . .

Both Advent and Lent carry penitential significance but for quite different reasons. Lenten preparation is targeted on the Resurrection of Jesus at Eastertime; it is a means of preparing us to welcome the hope and new life signified in the Easter event. Advent is a preparation to welcome Jesus back again, first by commemorating his original arrival in our midst two thousand years ago and second, to anticipate God's second coming at the end of time when God will finally sort out the mess the world is in. In both cases, the focus is on divine intervention, first to undo the power of sin on human life and second to bring a final end to this vale of tears so that we can all live happily with God forever thereafter.

Advent, therefore, marks a serious theological anomaly, reducing Incarnation to human need and benefit, viewing the human within an anthropology that is seriously distorted from both a human and divine perspective. The human is caught in both a time warp and an anthropological bottleneck into which God is insinuated in a rather bizarre piece of anthropocentric reductionism. Everything that has happened in the evolving and paradoxical grandeur of creation over several eons is bypassed, in fact demonized; only what happens after the time limit of two thousand years ago is of salvific importance. And as indicated in Chapter 5, humanity's own God-endowed, incarnational story, spreading over a time span of some seven million years, is also subverted.

All the emphasis on the waiting verges on blasphemous rhetoric. It is based on a kind of stark blindness of a species that has become so religiously convoluted that it is unable to behold the elegance staring us in the face. God's incarnational affirmation over a time span of seven million years is totally ignored, and because of the emphasis on the final coming (of God in judgment) the two-thousand-year-old understanding of Incarnation is also nullified; it does not really achieve what Christians claim it has achieved—so we must go on waiting!

For almost two thousand years, Christians have been the victims of a false utopia. Worse still it has—to varying degrees—rendered us ineffective in bringing about the transformation signaled by the historical Jesus in the project of the New Reign of God (the new companionship). We have been suffering from a kind of schizophrenic disempowerment, making us so guilt-ridden and unworthy, we are unable to muster the courage and wisdom to get on with the gospel empowerment that Jesus modelled for us. Instead, dysfunctional and paralyzed, we continue waiting for the redemptive patriarch beyond the sky to come to our rescue.

We need to grow up and do so rapidly! We have been endowed with all the incarnational blessings any species could hope for. First, we are born out of an organic thriving universe, earthed in a vibrant energetic planet, with a grace-filled story of some seven million years. On every side, we are blessed with multiple resources; if we would only wake up to what truly we are meant to be about. Advent and Christmas serve as perpetual reminders to us that we have been birthed from the womb of a birthing universe, in the enduring empowerment of the energetic Spirit. And our task is to continue the creative process of birthing anew the creation that has birthed us. That more than anything else is what Advent and Christmas are all about.

Chapter 11

Incarnational Education for Adults

When I was a child, I talked like a child, I thought like a child, I reasoned like a child. When I became an adult, I put the ways of childhood behind me.

—St. Paul (1 Cor 13:11)

I learned most not from those who taught me but from those who talked with me.

—St. Augustine

All over the world, religious adherents try to instill in young children a familiarity with their faith and a knowledge of the fundamentals to hold on to for life. I suspect that zealous religious educators would not be at all too pleased with the words of St. Paul, quoted above. Contrary to Paul's word, traditional Christianity has emphasized the need to cling to what you were given in childhood, and not allow it to be undermined by adult questioning or critique. It seems to me that neither in Christianity nor in world religion generally have we taken to heart Paul's admonition for an adult appropriation of faith.

The problem I am highlighting may be rooted in our popular understanding of education as a strategy of passing on information and wisdom from seniors to juniors, from the learned to the unlearned. Even in third-level institutes, a clear distinction prevails between those who hold the monopoly of wisdom and those who are there to receive it. While many educational programs today encourage and promote participation, and the empowerment of the student to do research for oneself, there is rarely any sense of an egalitarian playing field where teacher and student engage in a collaborative endeavor.

Malcolm Knowles (d.1997), one of the great pioneers of adult education in the United States, named the challenge of dealing with adults as one of *andragogy*, not *pedagogy* (1986).[1] At the adult level, the process is meant to be different and frequently fails to measure up to what many would consider to be the ideal. Such is the indoctrination of the top-down approach; it requires a concerted and concentrated effort to do things differently.

Throughout the latter half of the twentieth century, the notion of adult learning came to the fore. The primary goal is the mobilization of the wisdom garnered from life experience. The teacher is meant to be a facilitator for that process, whose main advantage over the pupil (or learner) is that the teacher has become more acquainted with the processing of life experience, her or his own and that of others.

The present chapter carries the ambitious title for seeking out those skills and strategies that will enable and empower the adult faith seeker to create or discover programs in adult faith development that are more conducive to the incarnational growth explored in the present book. There are few exemplary models to draw on, but programs associated with adult learning

---

[1] Andragogy is derived from the Greek *man-leading*, better understood in our time as human-centered. The term was originally used in 1833 by Alexander Kapp, a German educator. Malcom Knowles used the word in opposition to pedagogy, which he understood to be largely if not exclusively for children and teenagers. For a contemporary overview of Knowles's work and various applications to adult learning, see Knowles, Holton, and Swanson (2011).

in general provide a substantial body of wisdom from which we can distill strategies that are known to be more engaging and empowering for the adult faith seeker of our time.

A central feature of adult learning is the ability to mobilize the life experience that the adult is bringing to the learning process. Adults expect their life experience to be taken seriously and implicitly rather than explicitly; adult learners wish to build on what they have already learned through their various life engagements. So, attached to rationality and cerebral wisdom are many of our learning strategies and our theoretical approach to education in general; this switch to experiential learning requires considerable attention. To begin with, there are a number of unexamined assumptions that need to be highlighted.

Engaging Experience

Our dominant patriarchal culture has long been suspicious of experience, perceiving it to be an inferior mode of discernment compared with the employment of the rational mind in the rigorous process of objective scientific verification. For the dominant culture—especially in epistemology and metaphysics—the use of *reason* is the only reliable method that will guarantee enduring truth. Experience introduces feelings, emotions, intuition, imagination, factors in the human makeup that are slippery, mood determined, solipsistic, subjective, difficult to quantify (and therefore not easy to control), and devoid of the clarity and precision of the rational objective viewpoint.

The scientific method dictates most outcomes in conventional classrooms at all levels of formal learning. Consequently, the arts—the medium often adopted to express intuition and imagination—have long been viewed as an inferior body of wisdom, devoid of the cultural significance of science-related education. By the same token, many people of artistic skill struggle to establish a meaningful career and frequently live with a great deal of social and financial insecurity.

And for adults, experience is their chief source of self-identity. To youths, experience is something that happens to them (and is often taken for granted), whereas adults define themselves in terms of their unique experiences. An adult's experience tends to define who he or she is. So if an adult's experience is not respected and valued, it cannot be used as a resource for learning. Adults experience this omission as a denial of their experience and as a rejection of themselves as persons, which negatively affects learning.

Marianne Janack (2012) has undertaken a comprehensive study of the notion of experience, unraveling at length the rather cerebral and anthropocentric (human-centered) arguments of philosophers over the past few thousand years. Time and again, her plea is for a quality of agency that situates the person in the contextual web of the natural world, the relational focus frequently highlighted throughout the present work. In conclusion, she pleads for an understanding of experience as situated cognition, encapsulating the wisdom of a number of contemporary theorists on this subject—namely, Philip Robbins, Murat Aydede, Susan Hurley, Alva Noë, and others. Janack defends *situatedness* as a superior way to understand experience and knowledge. Exactly what is the nature of the thing that is situated? Exactly what is this thing situated in, and in what way? For Janack, the answers are clear. The situated subject requires a first-person analysis in order to guarantee agency and responsibility—above and beyond the rational environment that imposes constraints on what is experienced and on what can be known. The learner, as an active agent, is often bringing complex perspectives arising from a range of life experiences, and the adult-learning strategy needs to ensure that this life wisdom is engaged and fully embraced.

Janack's core argument is that humans are not merely rational individual beings who can figure things out through a predominantly cerebral process (of mind or brain), as philosophy largely suggests. Rather, we are creatures insinuated into a complex web of life, participation and mutuality being our default positions. And in our engagements with the natural world, along with all we learn through those organic interactions, we accumulate a way of knowing that involves a great deal more than mere rational acquaintance. We experience life simultaneously on several levels, including the physical, social, emotional, intellectual, and spiritual. For instance, a sense of awe and wonder does not arise merely as a cognitive response, but also includes emotional, intellectual, and spiritual (not necessarily religious in the formal sense) ingredients in our encounter with physicality (e.g., experiencing a beautiful sunset). Some people privatize such an awakening holding it for inner reflection (or, perhaps, for personal prayer), but most people exhibit a desire to share and explore socially or interpersonally the impact of such an experience.

Barbara Bassot (2015) provides a valuable guide on how we process and discern the meaning of our experience. She goes on to outline the ingredients of a reflective process that incorporates several dimensions of adult education enumerated below. The pioneering work of the Franciscan theologian Ilia Delio (2013, 2015) alerts us to the intense and complex impetus of evolution in our world today, requiring of us attention to a situational landscape with several evolving features for our consideration and discernment. For instance, we are bombarded with information from many angles, arousing our curiosity to levels previously unknown and creating widespread questioning of long-honored truths within economics, politics, social policy, and religion.

While millions around our world still have to live with daily drudgery, violence, and oppression, thus confining their experience to the darkness of excessive pain and suffering, there is nonetheless a much more widespread desire for liberty and release from all forms of imposed rigidity. And this new experiential yearning for such freedom leads to a range of reactions and responses along the emancipatory spectrum. No matter how limited or oppressed people may be in the contemporary world, once they learn of novel possibilities, no matter how far-fetched, the information-saturated culture of our time augments an emotional and intellectual drive to go for it and bring about a breakthrough, no matter how small it may be. For the greater part, our patriarchal political, social, and religious systems react negatively to this new-found freedom; it poses a threat to the powers that be, and therefore the typical response tends to be one of subversion or derision rather than affirmation or encouragement. From within this context, we detect across the contemporary world the emergence of a new adult breakthrough.

The Shift toward Interiority

Ever since the spiritual awakening of the 1960s, spiritual seekers of more mature years yearn for renewed contact with inner wisdom, the type through which they can connect with and discern the deeper significance of their life experience. Initially it resulted in a plethora of meditation practices, many grounded in the Yoga focus of the great Eastern spiritualties. Buddhist practitioners flocked to the west while vast number of Westerners went east. The Dalai Lama and Thich Nhat Hahn became leading spiritual guides, to be followed much later by Eric Tolle and the extensive interest today in *Mindfulness* (see https://en.wikipedia.org/wiki/Mindfulness).

Within mainline Christianity itself, centering prayer enjoyed a new revival, with Metropolitan Anthony Bloom, John Main, Thomas Keating, and Lawrence Freeman among its leading advocates. Karl Rahner advised that we either become mystics once more or largely miss out on the awakening that was happening all around us. Thus, spirituality above and beyond religion became the new controversial breakthrough (see Johnson and Ord 2012).

In these developments—and a range of others—adult faith seekers were losing confidence in external criteria of compliance and seeking to ground their faith in the values of stillness, silence, and interiority. Distrust of religious institutions, and their legal requirements for affiliation and fidelity, lost much meaning and appeal. Millions began to abandon the practice of formal religion, a pattern that continues to our own time. Outward, quantifiable allegiance was giving way to inner exploration, with few objective criteria guiding the search.

This tendency to trust experience, and bring it to the discerning context of peer affiliation (hence the language of soul mates, and kindred spirits) began to replace the former allegiance to institutional church with its reliance on dogma, moral directive, and clerical management. Revealed truth came to be associated more with inner inspiration than with external religious norms. Allegations of a new, misguided solipsism, relativism, and individualism were frequently voiced; paradoxically, such protest seems to have reinforced the new orientation rather than diminished its spread. None of the mainline religions (to the best of my knowledge) have yet come to terms with a new upsurge toward interiority with its characteristic fluid experiential grounding.

Most commentators seem to have missed (or misunderstood) the broad reach of this interior awakening. It is not a case of each person acting according to his or her own whim and fancy. Nor is it a solipsistic form of individualism whereby people shut themselves off from all external referents. To the contrary, many of these new spiritual seekers connect with a vast range of movements and organizations unfolding around this new awakening. They connect and communicate broadly; they attend workshops and conferences, participate in dialogical encounters, and occasionally contribute to the social activism (justice work). Many claim to believe in Jesus but not in the church, and it is at this juncture that the spiritual seekers tend to incur the disapproval and dismissal of people who claim to know more about the spiritual life than these seekers ever could.

John Philip Newell (2014) provides a valuable analysis of this new spiritual awakening, highlighting the fact that the emerging interiority is a great deal more complex (and profound) than many ecclesiastics or religionists are capable of discerning.

The inner search for meaning is rarely confined to individual fulfillment but often embraces a relational interconnectedness transcending all past dualistic conditioning. Inner meaning is experienced not merely within the individual person but as a relational
dynamic engaging person, culture, and even the organic web of
life itself. The sacred is perceived to be at work in all creation
beyond the former dualistic split between the sacred and the
secular. Newell envisages the new Christian awakening in the
twenty-first century, under the following eight headings:

- Coming back into relationship with the earth as sacred;
- Reconnecting with compassion as the ground of true
  relationship;
- Celebrating the light that is at the heart of all life;
- Reverencing the wisdom of other religious traditions;
- Rediscovering spiritual practice as the basis for
  transformation;
- Living the way of nonviolence among nations;
- Looking to the unconscious as the wellspring of new
  vision; and
- Following love as the seed force of new birth in our lives
  and world.

This list could be employed to describe the spirituality of the
Great Spirit as outlined in Chapter 3. And the growing body of
evidence for the empowering creativity that characterized our
ancient human ancestors exhibits several parallels. Are we witnessing an evolutionary recapitulation, whereby the yearning
for a new spiritual depth is inadvertently reconnecting us with
archetypal stirrings long suppressed and subdued by patriarchal
religion? Might this be another fertile example of the energizing
Spirit blowing where she wills—with a bewildering freedom and
creativity that upends all our sanctioned paradigms?[2]

---

[2] The spiritual upheaval of the twenty-first century is quite a complex
phenomenon, one aspect of which I am describing in the present section,

The living Spirit in every age seems to breathe forth a wisdom that is as baffling as it is pregnant with empowering hope! While we seek that wisdom from deep within, I suggest we cannot go too far wrong. But it does involve clearing away the clutter of accumulated knowledge and information. On several fronts that is another major challenge facing adult faith seekers today.

The Wise Shall Inherit . . .

Such is the impact of our information age, that many people feel bombarded and even overwhelmed by information. How does one keep up with it all? In fact, most people don't maintain a pace that allows for the integration of what they learn daily. And such is the barbarity and exploitive nature of much of what we view on television and other media; we are often left baffled on how to process such information and helpless to be able to do anything about it in a proactive way.

I also suggest we need to differentiate between *information* and *knowledge*. As used here, information describes what bombards our senses on a daily basis, some of which is pleasing and fulfilling of our desires, but much of which we instantly dismiss because we cannot take it in, and more of which we strive to hold on to amid increasing levels of frustration, irritability, and sensory distraction. In the midst of all this, we are often the gull-

---

namely, the search for a new interiority—a feature I detect in several adult seekers of our time. Numerically, this constitutes a minority rather than majority of *religious believers* and is predominantly a Western phenomenon. However, *I believe it is a movement of significant evolutionary import.* Two other movements require the discerning attention of our time, but these do not belong to the envisaged readership of this book: first, the rise of religious fundamentalism, noted in many contemporary mainline religions, characteristic of young adults particularly; and second, modern Pentecostalism, constituting the fastest-growing Christian denomination today, with enormous appeal for the poor and marginalized (and for some fundamentalist Christians) around the world.

ible victims of fiercely impressive advertising frequently dictating and controlling our consumerist desires. Throughout much of the modern world, we simply go along with it, with minimal awareness of the damage being done to the environment, to earthly and human resources, and to the growing gap around the world between rich and poor.

Knowledge shifts things up a gear. It is the intellectual and academic pursuit of causes and consequences that at least in theory should make us more aware. However, our knowledge is often controlled and mediated by powerful forces over which rank-and-file citizens have little or no control. Governments seek out and employ expertise in knowledge that will support and reinforce the policies they uphold, and these are frequently valued in terms of how much wealth they will accumulate. Knowledge therefore is often at the mercy of sinister and sophisticated power dynamics, leaving truth distorted and even unrecognizable.

Then we come to the third category, *wisdom*, the primary concern of the present work and the gift that wise elders can bring to our confused and greed-driven culture. Wisdom is not in conflict with either information or knowledge, but rather appropriates each in a much more discerning way. In terms of information, wisdom seeks to differentiate between constructive and destructive forms, useful and deleterious ways of employing information, learning the adaptations that can distinguish the violent from the nonviolent. In terms of knowledge, it employs a hermeneutic of suspicion seeking to identify the powers at work in what is being communicated and the collusions that ensue. For instance, in the United States alone for every 2.3 doctors, there is one pharmaceutical sales person, leaving every pressurized doctor strongly lured to offer the latest pharmaceutical panacea to the codependent patient.

Every human person is endowed with wisdom and gifted with intellect. Such, however, is the educational drivenness of our time that many people fail to distinguish between intellectual prowess and academic achievement. Frequently, we judge ourselves and each other by the letters after our names, by the degrees we have obtained from one university or the other. In themselves such attainments are no guarantee of healthy intellectual development or of elevated levels of wisdom. We often encounter people with relatively little formal education, whose practical skill and intellectual savviness leave an enduring impression. Wisdom is often defined by its own innate potential; in gospel language, by their fruits you shall know them.

The wise elders of our time stand out precisely for this innate wisdom through which they tend to read reality differently, offering challenges for truth and credibility that can have substantial consequences. And not infrequently, they are the people from whom we would not expect this outcome, nor is their wisdom received hospitably in a world so fixated on rational discourse. To the contrary, they are often shunned, derided, and even ridiculed.

The Adult Forum

What therefore are the channels—and structures—needed to mobilize this emancipatory consciousness of our time? We need forums in which elders (and others) can hear each other out. And the elders themselves need outlets that will channel and advance their deepening sense of wisdom. What might adult pedagogy look like in practice? What strategies would be congenial to liberate the desired outcomes experienced by adults today?

Simply enter "Adult Learning/Education" in your computer search engine and you will encounter a vast range of webpages. Most if not all will refer to the pioneering work of Malcolm Knowles whose *Andragogy Principles* have been adapted and further refined by specialists in adult learning. These principles include the following:

- The motivation for the adult learner is internal rather than external.
- Learning is fundamentally social, a principle not easily implemented in an educational culture focused more on the individual, with frequent recourse to online resources.
- Knowledge is integrated in the life of communities, especially those coparticipants around whom our experience of life has been molded.
- The depth of our learning depends on the depth of our engagement. The more we are actively involved, the more we learn.
- Engagement is joined at the hip with empowerment. Adults perceive their identities in terms of their ability to contribute.
- WIIFM (what's in it for me) is critical. Relevance for our daily lives is crucial.
- The big picture is first, then the details, which should support the ideals of the big picture.
- Where does this new learning fit in relation to the other stuff I know? Adults like to be able to connect with what they already know. They learn best by ongoing process of their lived experience.
- Adults are problem centered rather than content oriented.
- Since vision and hearing decline with the aging process, closer attention to the learning environment of adults is required.
- Since short-term memory decreases with age, repetition increases our retention of critical information.
- Adults need to be involved in bringing about the desired outcomes of their learning, and this is best achieved through regular dialogue.

Increasingly, adult learning, like that of younger age groups, will involve a range of online resources requiring computer and technological skills more familiar to younger people. Evidence shows, however, that older people can also learn these skills within an appropriate supportive environment. Christopher Pappas, founder of the eLearning Industry's Network (the largest online community of professionals involved in the eLearning Industry) has drawn up the following guidelines, some of which overlap with those listed above:

- Adult learners need to be able to see the relevancy of what they are learning.
- Include activities and assignments that encourage adult learners to explore. Adult learners accumulate knowledge most effectively when they are active participants in their own learning process.
- Consider the experience and educational background of the adult learners. Adult learners have typically gathered more life experience and accumulated a broader knowledge.
- Offer immediate feedback to allow adult learners to learn from mistakes and how best to explore alternative problem solving approaches.
- Integrate emotionally driven content. When adults feel emotionally connected to the subject matter, they are more likely to absorb and retain the information.
- Emphasize the real-world benefits and especially applications to daily life situations.
- Keep cognitive overload in mind when creating content. Avoid using large blocks of text, and opt for bullet points or numbered lists instead.
- Use avatars and storytelling to draw forth the wisdom of adult learners.
- Create online resources that can be accessed quickly and conveniently.
- Use aesthetically pleasing design elements—more interactive and visually stimulating—to enhance the learning experience.

In adult learning, the teacher has to become a resource person and facilitator of a learning experience in which the learner becomes an active participant. To that end, one needs to create a safe, welcoming environment, characterized by a culture of empathy, respect, approachability, and authenticity. All strategies need to embody a transparent sense of collaboration, and outcomes need to be evaluated in terms of practical value to the learner. As noted earlier, sensory abilities can weaken with increasing age, requiring more careful attention to the integration of visual, auditory, and tactile elements in the learning environment.

Teachers should provide autonomy and independence. This can mean the freedom of pace, choice, method, content, or assessment, conducive to the inner motivation that tends to characterize adult learners. For instance, learners "should be free to work at their own speed, choose to study particular aspects of a course, adopt whatever learning style suits them best, and be free to choose what they learn" (Jarvis 2004, 154). Teaching should empower learners. As a corollary to the need to provide autonomy and independence, teachers should share power and decision-making roles with their adult learners. Teachers should not feel obliged to provide right answers. They should make sure that there is equal access to all resources, include self-evaluation in graded courses, involve learners in managing the learning environment, and be open and explicit about what is happening and why (see Rubenson 2011, 57).

Adult Formation in Church Context

Throughout most of the Christian world, churches and Christian denominations devote substantial resources to the faith development of children and juniors. Many still operate out of the conviction that the more we can indoctrinate them in their youth, the better are the chances that they will retain such wisdom for life and use it in the practice of their faith. The outcome clearly proves the opposite. Most Christian faith communities, despite zealous attempts by parents, creative endeavors by teachers, and attractive liturgies in churches, fail to hold on to youth, who during various stages throughout adolescence drift away, and abandon church entirely by their early twenties.

Christian educational systems still seem to be clinging to the earlier developmental psychology that claimed that life-long wisdom needs to be in place by the end of the adolescent period, because it cannot be acquired thereafter (in a meaningful or integrated way). We now know that substantial learning, and developmental adjustments, can, and do, take place throughout later life stages. We also know that a more mature appropriation of faith belongs to the adult stages than to childhood or adolescence. Acknowledging this new development, some church and faith communities have set up programs within churches and parishes on adult faith formation. An American Dominican Sister, Janet Schaeffler, provides valuable guidelines and a range of published resources on her website www.janetschaeffler.com.

In 2002, the conference of Catholic Bishops in the United States published a document, *Our Hearts Were Burning Within Us: A Pastoral Plan for Adult Faith Formation in the United States.* This became the basis for a number of programs throughout the United States seeking to evangelize Catholics into a more informed understanding of Catholic faith according to the Catechism of the Catholic Church. While highlighting the need for an adult understanding of faith (above and beyond what was required for children), its rather narrow Catholic focus, and an underling agenda of incorporating Catholics into greater fidelity to the church itself, it failed to address the evolving religious and spiritual questions of the twenty-first century and increasingly came to be seen as of little value for the kind of adult formation envisaged in the present work.

Education in adult faith development can no longer be reserved to churches or denominational settings. Contemporary adult faith seekers distrust all major institutions, including churches

and religions. Adults in our time seek spiritual wisdom and guidance in a range of other contexts, notably at conferences, workshops, third-level institutes, informal reading or study groups,
in retreat centers, and individually through spiritual accompani-
ment or through spiritually based counseling. Sometimes they
find what they are seeking, but frequently, it can be a long and
lonely search. They know what does not satisfy, but seeking an
alternative that will prove fulfilling and enriching often results in
a spiritual vacuum not easily filled.

My hope is that the reflections of this book, and the practical
suggestions of the present chapter, will provide animation and
encouragement toward incarnational growth for the growing
cohort of contemporary adults seeking renewed faith and hope
in the evolving context of the twenty-first century.

Bibliography

Abram, David. 1996. *The Spell of the Sensuous*. New York: Random House.

_____. 2010. *Becoming Animal: An Earthly Cosmology*. New York: Vintage Books.

Aisworth, Claire. 2015. "Sex Redefined." *Nature* 518: 288–91.

Alesina, Alberto, et al. 2013. "On the Origins of Gender Roles: Women and the Plough." *Quarterly Journal of Economics* 128: 469–530.

Arnett, Jeffrey. 2014. *Emerging Adulthood: The Winding Road from the Late Teens through the Twenties*, 2nd ed. New York: Oxford University Press.

Atchley, Robert C. 2009. *Spirituality and Aging*. Baltimore: Johns Hopkins University Press.

Avis, Paul. 1989. *Eros and the Sacred*. London: SPCK.

Barker, Graeme. 2006. *The Agricultural Revolution in Prehistory*. Oxford: Oxford University Press.

Bassot, Barbara. 2015. *The Reflective Practice Guide: An Interdisciplinary Approach to Critical Reflection*. New York: Routledge.

Baumeister, Dayna. 2014. *Biomimicry Resource Handbook: A Seed Bank of Best Practices* North Charleston, SC: CreateSpace.

Benyus, Janine M. 2002. *Biomimicry: Innovation Inspired by Nature*. London: HarperCollins Perennials.

Bevans, Stephen. 2009. *An Introduction to Theology in Global Perspective*. Maryknoll, NY: Orbis Books.

Black, Peter. 2003. "The Broken Wings of Eros." *Theological Studies* 64: 106–26.

Blaffer Hrdy, Sarah. 2009. *Mothers and Others: The Evolutionary Origins of Mutual Understanding.* Cambridge MA: Harvard University Press.

Boehm, Christopher. 1999. *Hierarchy in the Forest.* Cambridge, MA: Harvard University Press.

———. 2012. *Moral Origins.* New York: Basic Books.

Boff, Leonardo. 1995. *Ecology and Liberation: A New Paradigm.* Maryknoll, NY: Orbis Books.

———. 2015. *Come Holy Spirit!* Maryknoll, NY: Orbis Books.

Borg, Marcus, and John Dominic Crossan. 2007. *The First Christmas.* New York: Harper One.

Bourgeault, Cynthia. 2010. *The Meaning of Mary Mgdalene.* Boston: Shambala.

Bowles, Samuel, and Herbert Gintis. 2013. *A Cooperative Species: Human Reciprocity and Its Evolution.* Princeton, NJ: Princeton University Press.

Braidotti, Rosi. 2014. *The Posthuman.* Cambridge: Polity Press.

Brett, Gregory. 2013. *The Theological Notion of the Human Person.* New York: Peter Lang.

Brock, Rita N. 1992. *Journeys by Heart: A Christology of Erotic Power.* New York: Crossroad.

Budin, Stephanie Lynn. 2008. *The Myth of Sacred Prostitution in Antiquity.* New York: Cambridge University Press.

Butler, Judith. 1990. *Gender Trouble.* New York: Routledge.

———. 2004. *Undoing Gender.* New York: Routledge.

Byers, Andrew. 2013. *TheoMedia: The Media of God in the Digital Age.* Eugene, OR: Cascade Books.

Calaprice, Alice. 2005. *The New Quotable Einstein.* Princeton, NJ: Princeton University Press.

Campbell, Charlie. 2013. *Scapegoat: A History of Blaming Other People.* London: Duckworth.

Cannato, Judy. 2006. *Radical Amazement.* Notre Dame, IN: Sorin Books.

———. 2010. *Field of Compassion.* Notre Dame, IN: Sorin Books.

Christ, Carol P. 2016. "A New Definition of Patriarchy: Control of Women's Sexuality, Private Property, and War." *Feminist Theology*, 24: 214–25.

Christie, Douglas. 2013. *The Blue Sapphire of the Mind.* New York: Oxford University Press.

Cole-Turner, Ronald. 2016. "Eschatology and the Technologies of Human Advancement." *Interpretation* 70: 21–33.

Conway Morris, Simon. 2003. *Life's Solution: Inevitable Humans in a Lonely Universe*. New York: Cambridge University Press.

Cook, Jill. 2013. *Ice Age Art—Arrival of the Modern Mind*. London: British Museum Press.

Cook-Greuter, Susanne. 1994. *Transcendence and Mature Thought in Adulthood*. Lanham, MD: Rowman & Littlefield.

_____. 1999. *Postautonomous Ego Development: A Study of Its Nature and Measurement*. PhD diss., Harvard University Graduate School of Education.

Cooper, Kate. 2013. *Band of Angels: The Forgotten World of Early Christian Women*. New York: Overlook Press.

Copan, Paul. 2007. *Loving Wisdom: Christian Philosophy of Religion*. St. Louis, MO: Chalice Press.

Crossan, John Dominic. 1991. *The Historical Jesus*. San Francisco: HarperSanFrancisco.

_____. 1996. *Who Is Jesus?* New York: HarperCollins.

_____. 2010. *The Greatest Prayer*. New York: HarperCollins.

Davies, Paul. 2006. *The Goldilocks Enigma: Why Is the Universe Just Right for Life?* London: Penguin.

Dawkins, Richard. 2006. *The God Delusion*. London: Bantam.

Deane-Drummond, Celia. 2014. *The Wisdom of the Liminal*. Grand Rapids, MI: Eerdmans.

Delio, Ilia. 2013. *The Unbearable Wholeness of Being*. Maryknoll, NY: Orbis Books.

_____. 2015. *Making All Things New: Catholicity, Cosmology, Consciousness*. Maryknoll, NY: Orbis Books.

De Waal, Frans. 2010. *The Age of Empathy*. New York: Random House.

Dulles, Avery. 1983. *Models of Revelation*. Maryknoll, NY: Orbis Books.

Dunnill, John. 2013. *Sacrifice and the Body*. New York: Routledge.

Eagleton, Terry. 2010. *On Evil*. New Haven, CT: Yale University Press.

Ettinger, Bracha. 2006. *The Matrixial Borderspace*. Minneapolis: University of Minnesota Press.

Farley, Margaret A. 2007. *Just Love: A Framework for Christian Sexual Ethics*. New York: Continuum.

Farley, Wendy. 2011. *Gathering Those Driven Away: A Theology of Incarnation*. Louisville, KY: WJK Press.

Fausto-Sterling, Anne. 2012. *Sex/Gender: Biology in a Social World.* New York: Routledge.

Feehan, John. 2012. *The Singing Heart of the World.* Maryknoll, NY: Orbis Books.

Formosa, M. 2009. "Renewing Universities of the Third Age: Challenges and Visions for the Future." *Recerca* 9: 171–96.

———. 2010. "Lifelong Learning in Later Life: The Universities of the Third Age". *Lifelong Learning Institute Review* 5: 1–12.

Fowler, James. 1981. *Stages of Faith.* San Francisco: Harper & Row.

Fox, Matthew. 1983. *Original Blessing: A Primer in Creation Spirituality.* Santa Fe, NM: Bear.

Fox, Patricia. 2001. *God as Communion.* Collegeville, MN: Liturgical Press.

Fry, Douglas P., and Patrik Soderberg. 2014. "Myths about Hunter-gatherers Redux: Nomadic Foragers, War and Peace." *Journal of Aggression, Conflict and Peace Research* 6: 255–66.

Funk, Robert. 1996. *Honest to Jesus.* San Francisco: HarperSanFrancisco.

Giddens, Anthony. 1985. *The Nation-State and Violence.* Cambridge: Polity Press.

———. 1992. *The Transformation of Intimacy.* Cambridge: Polity Press.

Girard, Rene. 1986. *The Scapegoat.* Baltimore: Johns Hopkins University Press.

Goehring, James E. 1999. *Ascetics, Society and the Desert.* Harisburg, PA: Trinity Press International.

Gould, Stephen J. 1994. "The Evolution of Life on Earth." *Scientific American* 271: 62–69.

Goosen, Gideon. 2011. *Hyphenated Christians.* New York: Peter Lang.

Habel, Norman. 1995. *The Land Is Mine.* Minneapolis, MN: Augsburg Fortress.

Harman, Jay. 2014. *The Shark's Paintbrush: Biomimicry and How Nature Is Inspiring Innovation.* Ashland, OR: White Cloud Press.

Hart, Donna, and Robert Sussman. 2005. *Man the Hunted.* New York: Basic Books.

Haughey, John C. 2015. *A Biography of the Spirit.* Maryknoll, NY: Orbis Books.

Haught, John F. 2010. *Making Sense of Evolution*. Louisville, KY: Westminster/John Knox Press.

_____. 2015. *Resting on the Future*. New York: Bloomsbury.

Heinrich, Bernd. 2013. *Life Everlasting: The Animal Way of Death*. New York: Mariner Books.

Hick, John. 1995. *A Christian Theology of Religions: The Rainbow of Faiths*. Louisville, KY: Westminster John Knox.

Hill, Jason D. 2000. *Becoming a Cosmopolitan*. Lanham, MD: Rowman & Littlefield.

Howard-Brook, Wes. 2010. *Come Out My People!: God's Call Out of Empire in the Bible and Beyond*. Maryknoll, NY: Orbis Books.

_____. 2016: *Empire Baptized: How the Church Embraced What Jesus Rejected*. Maryknoll, NY: Orbis Books.

Isherwood, Lisa. 2006. *The Power of Erotic Celibacy*. Edinburgh: T. & T. Clark.

_____, (with David Harris). 2013. *Radical Otherness*. London: Routledge.

Janack, Marianne. 2012. *What We Mean by Experience*. Redwood City, CA: Stanford University Press.

Jantzen, Grace. 1995. *Power, Gender and Christian Mysticism*. Cambridge: Cambridge University Press.

Jarvis, P. 2004. *Adult Education and Lifelong Learning*. London: Falmer Press.

Johnson, Elizabeth. 2004. *Truly Our Sister*. New York: Continuum.

_____. 2014. *Ask the Beasts!* New York: Bloomsbury.

Johnson, Kurt, and David R. Ord. 2012. *The Coming Inter-spiritual Age*. Vancouver: Namaste.

Keenan, Marie. 2011. *Child Sex Abuse and the Catholic Church*. Oxford: Oxford University Press.

Kelly, Anthony J. 2015. "Human Consciousness, God and Creation." *Pacifica: Australasian Theological Studies* 28: 3–22.

Kennedy, Eugene. 2001. *The Unhealed Wound: The Church and Human Sexuality*. New York: St. Martin's Press.

Kim, Grace Ji-Sun. 2011. *The Holy Spirit, Chi, and the Other*. New York: Palgrave Macmillan.

Kimble, Melvin, and Susan H. McFadden. 1995/2003. *Handbook on Aging, Spirituality, and Religion*, vols. 1 and 2. Minneapolis, MN: Fortress/Augsburg Press.

Knowles, Malcolm. 1986. *The Adult Learner: A Neglected Species*. Houston, TX: Gulf.

Knowles, Malcolm, Elwood F. Holton III, and Richard A. Swanson. 2011. *The Adult Learner*, 7th ed. Oxford: Elsevier.

Koestler, Arthur. 1967. *The Ghost in the Machine*. New York: Penguin.

Kraay, Klaas J. 2014. *God and the Multiverse*. New York: Routledge.

Kripal, Jeffrey John. 2001. *Roads of Excess, Palaces of Wisdom: Eroticism and Reflexivity in the Study of Mysticism*. Chicago: University of Chicago Press.

Kurzweil, Ray. 2005. *The Singularity Is Near*. New York: Viking.

La Cugna, Catherine Mowry. 1991. *God for Us*. San Francisco: HarperSanFrancisco.

Lanzetta, Beverley. 2005. *Radical Wisdom: A Feminist Mystical Theology*. Minneapolis, MN: Augsburg Fortress Press.

_____. 2015. *Path of the Heart: A Spiritual Guide to Divine Union*. San Diego, CA: Blue Sapphire Books.

Lee, Dora. 2011. *Biomimicry: Inventions Inspired by Nature*. Toronto: Kids Can Press.

Lee, R. B., et al. 1968. *Man the Hunter*. Chicago: Aldine.

LeRon Shults, F. 2014. *Theology after the Birth of God: Atheist Conceptions in Cognition and Culture*. New York: Palgrave-Macmillan.

Lewis-Williams, David. 2002. *The Mind in the Cave*. London: Thames & Hudson.

Liebert, Elizabeth. 2015. *The Soul of Discernment*. Louisville, KY: WJK Press.

Lovelock, James. 1979. *Gaia: A New Look at Life on Earth*. New York: Oxford University Press.

_____. 1988. *The Ages of Gaia*. New York: Oxford University Press.

Lyons, Kathleen. 2015. *Mysticism and Narcissism*, Newcastle upon Tyne, UK: Cambridge Scholars.

MacKenzie, Catriona, and Natalie Stoljar. 2000. *Relational Autonomy: Feminist Perspectives on Autonomy, Agency, and Social Self*. New York: Oxford University Press.

Malone, Mary T. 2014. *The Elephant in the Church*. Dublin: Columba Press.

Manning, Richard. 2004. *Against the Grain: How Agriculture Has Hijacked Civilization*. New York: North Point Press.

Mannion, Gerard, ed. 2015. *Where We Dwell in Common: The Quest for Dialogue in the 21st Century.* New York: Palgrave Macmillan.

Margulis, Lynn. 1998. *The Symbiotic Planet.* New York: Basic Books.

_____. 2008. *Dazzle Gradually: Reflections on the Nature of Nature.* White River Junction, VT: Chelsea Green.

Masika-Lees, Frances. E. 2009. *Gender and Difference in a Globalizing World.* Long Grove, IL: Waveland Press.

Meredith, Martin. 2011. *Born in Africa.* London: Simon & Schuster.

Miller, Richard. 2010. *God, Creation and Climate Change.* Maryknoll, NY: Orbis Books.

Mithen, Steven. 1990. *Thoughtful Foragers.* Cambridge: Cambridge University Press.

Montgomery, Kathleen, ed. 2015. *Landscapes of Aging and Spirituality.* Boston: Skinner House Books.

Moore, Thomas. 1998. *The Soul of Sex.* New York: HarperCollins.

Morowitz, Harold J. 2002. *The Emergence of Everything: How the World Became Complex.* New York: Oxford University Press.

Moss, Candida. 2013. *The Myth of Persecution.* New York: HarperCollins.

Nelson, James B. 1992. *The Intimate Connection.* Louisville, KY: Westminster John Knox Press.

Nelson-Becker, Holly. 2009. "Exploring We Will Go: The Investigation of Religion and Spirituality in Older Populations." *Journal of Religion, Spirituality, & Aging* 21: 259–67.

_____. 2011. "Research in Spirituality, Religion, and Aging: An Emerging Area." *Generations Review,* http://www.britishgerontology.org/DB/gr-editions-2/generations-review/research-in-spirituality-religion-and-aging-an-eme.html.

Newell, John Philip. 2014. *The Rebirthing of God.* New York: Turner.

O'Connell, James. 2002. "Male Strategies and Plio-Pleistocene Archaeology." *Journal of Human Evolution.* 43: 831–72.

Ohmae, Kenichi. 1990. *The Borderless World.* London: Collins.

O'Murchu, Diarmuid. 2002. *Evolutionary Faith.* Maryknoll, NY: Orbis Books.

_____. 2008. *Ancestral Grace.* Maryknoll, NY: Orbis Books.

_____. 2010. *Adult Faith.* Maryknoll, NY: Orbis Books.

_____. 2011. *Christianity's Dangerous Memory.* New York: Crossroad.

_____. 2012. *In the Beginning Was the Spirit*. Maryknoll, NY: Orbis Books.

_____. 2014a. *On Being a Postcolonial Christian*. North Charleston, SC: CreateSpace.

_____. 2014b. *The Meaning and Practice of Faith*. Maryknoll, NY: Orbis Books.

_____. 2015. *Inclusivity: A Gospel Mandate*. Maryknoll, NY: Orbis Books.

Oppenheimer, Stephen. 2003. *The Real Eve: Modern Man's Journey Out of Africa*. New York: Basic Books.

Osiek, Carolyn, and Margaret MacDonald. 2006. *A Woman's Place: House Churches in Earliest Christianity*. Minneapolis, MN: Fortress Press.

Page, Nick. 2012. *The Wrong Messiah*. London: Hodder & Stoughton.

Panikkar, Raimon. 2006. *The Experience of God*. Minneapolis, MN: Fortress Press.

Patterson, Stephen J. 2004. *Beyond the Passion: Rethinking the Death and Life of Jesus*. Minneapolis, MN: Augsburg Fortress.

_____. 2014. *The Lost Way: How Two Forgotten Gospels Are Rewriting the Story of Christian Origins*. New York: HarperOne.

Pevny, Ron. 2014. *Conscious Living, Conscious Aging*. New York: Atria Paperback.

Phan, Peter. 2004. *Being Religious Interreligiously*. Maryknoll, NY: Orbis Books.

Phipps, Carter. 2012. *Evolutionaries*. New York: Harper Perennial.

Plotkin, Bill. 2008. *Nature and the Human Soul*. Novata, CA: New World Library.

Primark, Joel, and Nancy Abrams. 2006. *The View from the Center of the Universe*. New York: Riverhead Books.

Pugh, Ben. 2015. *Atonement Theories*. Eugene, OR: Wipf and Stock.

Rahner, Karl. 1968. *Spirit in the World*. New York: Herder & Herder.

_____. 1969. *Grace in Freedom*. New York: Herder & Herder.

_____. 1978. *Foundations of Christian Faith*. New York: Seabury Press.

Raiser, K. 1991. *Ecumenism in Transition: A Paradigm Shift in the Ecumenical Movement?* Geneva: WCC Publications.

Reid-Bowen, Paul. 2007. *Goddess as Nature*. Burlington, VT: Ashgate.

Renfrew, Colin, et al. 2009. *The Sapient Mind: Archaeology Meets Neuroscience*. New York: Oxford University Press.

Renfrew, Colin, and Michael J. Boyd. 2016. *Death Rituals, Social Order and the Archaeology of Immortality in the Ancient World*. New York: Cambridge University Press.

Ridley, Matt. 1996. *The Origins of Virtue*. London: Viking.

Rifkin, Jeremy. 2010. *The Empathic Civilization*. Cambridge: Polity Press.

Roszak, Theodore. 2001. *The Longevity Revolution*. Berkeley, CA: Berkeley Hills Books.

_____. 2009. *The Making of an Elder Culture*. Gabriola Island, BC: New Society.

Roughgarden, Joan. 2009. *Evolution's Rainbow*. Oakland, CA: University of California Press.

Rovelli C. 1996. "Relational Quantum Mechanics." *International Journal of Theoretical Physics* 35: 1637–78.

Rubenstein, Mary-Jane. 2014. *Worlds without End: The Many Lives of the Multiverse*. New York: Columbia University Press.

Rubenson, K. 2011. *Adult Learning and Education*. Oxford: Academic Press.

Ryan, Christopher, and Cacilda Jethá. 2010. *Sex at Dawn*. New York: HarperCollins.

Saxon, Lynn. 2012. *Sex at Dusk*. Self-published.

Schaberg, Jane. 1987. *The Illegitimacy of Jesus*. San Francisco: Harper & Row.

Schaefer, Donovan O. 2015. *Religious Affects: Animality, Evolution, and Power*. Durham, NC: Duke University Press.

Schafer, Lothar. 2013. *Infinite Potential: What Quantum Physics Reveals*. New York: Random House.

Seabright, Paul. 2012. *The War of the Sexes: How Conflict and Cooperation Have Shaped Men and Women from Prehistory to the Present*. Princeton, NJ: Princeton University Press.

Sipe, Richard. 1995. *Sex, Priests and Power*. New York: Routledge.

Sorokim, Petrim. 1950. *Modern Historical and Social Philosophies*. New York: Dover Publications.

Spencer, Daniel T. 1996. *Gay and Gaia: Ethics, Ecology and the Erotic*. Cleveland, OH: Pilgrim Press.

Spiller, C., and Rachel Wolfgramm, eds. 2015. *Indigenous Spiritualities at Work*. Charlotte, NC: Information Age.

Spong, John Shelby. 2007. *Jesus for Non-Religious*. San Francisco: HarperSanFrancisco.

_____. 2016. *Biblical Literalism: A Gentile Heresy*. New York: Harper One.

Stewart, John. 2000. *Evolution's Arrow: The Direction of Evolution and the Future of Humanity.* Canberra, Australia: Chapman Press.

Stokes, Ken, ed. 1982. *Faith in the Adult Life Cycle*, New York: W. H. Sadlier.

Stout, Dietrich. 2016. "Tales of a Stone Age Neuroscientist." *Scientific American* 314: 21–27.

Swimme, Brian, and Thomas Berry. 1992. *The Universe Story.* New York: Penguin.

_____, and Mary Evelyn Tucker. 2011. *Journey of the Universe.* New Haven, CT: Yale University Press.

Tamez, Elsa. 2007. *Struggles for Power in Early Christianity.* Maryknoll, NY: Orbis Books.

United Nations. 2015. *World Population Prospects: The 2015 Revision Key Findings and Advance Tables,* https://esa.un.org/unpd/wpp/publications/files/key_findings_wpp_2015.pdf.

Taylor, Steve. 2005. *The Fall. Winchester*, UK: O Books.

Volf, Miroslav. 1996. *Exclusion and Embrace.* Nashville, TN: Abingdon Press.

Wallace, Mark. 2005. *Finding God in the Singing River.* Minneapolis, MN: Fortress Press.

Walter, Chip. 2013. *The Last Ape Standing: The Seven Million Year Story.* New York: Random House.

Weber, Robert L., and Carol Orsborn. 2015. *The Spirituality of Age.* Rochester, VT: Park St. Press.

White, George W. 2007. *Nation, State and Territory: Origins, Evolutions and Relationships.* Lanham, MD: Rowman & Littlefield.

Wink, Walter. 2002. *The Human Being: Jesus and the Enigma of the Son of Man.* Minneapolis, MN: Augsburg Fortress.

Wirzba, Norman. 2011. *Food and Faith: A Theology of Eating.* New York: Cambridge University Press.

Wright, Robert. 2000. *Nonzero: History, Evolution and Human Cooperation.* London: Abacus.

Wright-Knust, Jennifer. 2011. *Unprotected Texts: The Bible's Surprising Contradictions about Sex and Desire.* New York: HarperOne.

Young Lee, Jung. 1996. *The Trinity in Asian Perspective.* Nashville, TN: Abingdon Press.

Zihlman, Adrienne. 2012. "The Real Females of Human Evolution." *Evolutionary Anthropology* 21: 270–76.

Index